Related Kaplan Titles

John Douglas's Guide to the Police Exam, Second Edition
John Douglas's Guide to the California Police Exam

Guide to Careers in the FBI
Second Edition

by John Douglas

Simon & Schuster

NEW YORK · LONDON · SYDNEY · TORONTO

Kaplan Publishing
Published by SIMON & SCHUSTER
Rockefeller Center
1230 Avenue of the Americas
New York, NY 10020

Editorial Director: Jennifer Farthing
Project Editor: Sheryl Gordon
Production Manager: Michael Shevlin
Content Manager: Patrick Kennedy
Page Layout: Baldur Gudbjornsson
Cover Design: Mark Weaver

Manufactured in the United States of America.
Published simultaneously in Canada.

10 9 8 7 6 5 4 3 2 1

October 2005

ISBN-13: 978-0-7432-7280-3
ISBN-10:   0-7432-7280-3

For information regarding special discounts for bulk purchases, please contact Simon & Schuster Special Sales at 1-800-456-6798 or business@simonandschuster.com.

CONTENTS

ABOUT THE AUTHOR

During 25 years with the FBI, **John Douglas** became a leading expert on criminal personality profiling. Early in his career, he served as a recruiter for the Bureau; later, he conducted the first organized study into the methods and motivations of serial criminals, and became known as the pioneer of modern criminal investigative analysis. As a consultant, he continues assisting in criminal investigations and prosecutions throughout the world. An Air Force veteran, Douglas holds a doctorate in adult education, and is the author of numerous articles and presentations on criminology. He coauthored two landmark criminology texts: *Sexual Homicide: Patterns and Motives* and the *Crime Classification Manual*. With Mark Olshaker, he's coauthored several best-selling nonfiction books: *Mindhunter: Inside the FBI's Elite Serial Crime Unit; Unabomber: On the Trail of America's Most-Wanted Serial Killer; Journey into Darkness: The FBI's Premier Investigator Penetrates the Minds and Motives of the Most Terrifying Serial Killers;* and *Obsession: The FBI's Legendary Profiler Probes the Psyches of Killers, Rapists and Stalkers, and Their Victims, and Tells How to Fight Back.* He lives in the Washington DC area.

DEDICATION

This book is dedicated to all FBI Special Agents—past, present, and future—who make the ultimate sacrifice in the line of duty.

ACKNOWLEDGMENTS

I'd like to thank all the former Special Agents who shared their insights and expertise; this book could never have been written without their generosity and good humor. Paula Klaris deserves special thanks for her invaluable editorial assistance.

In 1977, **Katherine M. Newbold** received an appointment to the FBI Academy as one of the Bureau's first 100 women agents. She followed in the footsteps of her father, who presented her with FBI credentials in May 1978. She spent the balance of her investigative career on multi-agency drug task forces in New York City directed at Sicilian Mafia and Colombian transnational drug enterprises and violent street gangs. Newbold holds a doctorate in Criminal Justice from City University of New York with a concentration in psychology and sociology. Her final years with the FBI were spent as a Supervisor covering 14 divisions. Newbold retired from the FBI in 2002, and is now a consultant with XG Consultants Group, Inc. of New York City. She is also an adjunct professor at Illinois Valley Community College. Newbold lives in Central Illinois.

PART ONE
Introduction to the FBI

CHAPTER 1

Best Work In Law Enforcement

You are going to get a lot of just-the-facts-ma'am information in this book. You are also going to get a look at just what it's like to be a member of what I consider the finest investigative agency in the world. The information here comes from the Bureau itself and from the experts—former FBI Special Agents.

This book differs from most career planning guides. This is about a passion that was my career for over 25 years and about what I consider to be the best work in law enforcement. Included are facts and solid advice to help you evaluate your edge as a competitive candidate for a career in the Federal Bureau of Investigvation, both in sworn positions and in the numerous professional positions tied to the FBI mission.

Even the most casual follower of current events is aware of the changes that have affected law enforcement since the September 11 attacks in 2001. The FBI now has an even more extraordinary presence overseas involving investigators, Evidence Response Teams, Bomb and Explosive Experts, and Forensic Scientists in both the physical and behavioral fields. Critical Incident Response Teams, Hostage Resuce and Swat Teams, Cyberspace Experts, and Language Specialists also make up the nuts and bolts of the FBI—field investigators and analysts present only a glimpse at FBI opportunities. Just remember, the ever-changing mission, the fast pace, and the unbreakable camaraderie make the FBI a very gratifying career.

The Bureau has come a very long way since my Entered-on–Duty (EOD in Bureau-ese) in the late '60s. Then, the Bureau recruited only men for its Special Agent position, and it referred to other in-house professionals as "support staff." But the Bureau is a microcosm of society and has adjusted accordingly. The organization has made a large effort to change the composition of its workforce and to respect and recognize the contributions of all FBI personnel. In 1972, the Bureau began appointing women to agent positions, and they have been a vital presence ever since. Through the years, the Bureau has also changed with respect to technology and investigative response capability.

This book will give you insight into the extensive history behind the FBI. You will learn about the hierarcy within the organization, and read in detail about the myriad of task forces and programs the FBI takes part in every day. Each chapter is peppered with first-hand accounts of on-the-job experiences by former Special Agents.

You will then find out exactly what a career with the FBI entails, and precisely the types of candidates the Bureau looks for. We will walk together through the application process. By the time you have finished reading, I am sure you will have an idea whether or not a career with the FBI is right for you.

FIRST-HAND ACCOUNTS

Before we begin our adventure, I want you to read some of the first-hand stories from individuals I respect both personally and professionally. They are designed to assist you in honestly evaluating both the career and the application process. These people represent the heart and expertise of the FBI. Perhaps you will recognize yourself in their backgrounds and stories. Through their experiences, you will discover the range of opportunities available with the FBI and a "walk in my shoes" candor as presented in no other text. The FBI is clearly about making important contributions on a transnational stage. Many FBI colleagues have often said "where else can I get paid for doing this?"

I'm giving you their stories here for two reasons. First, you'll see a range of the career opportunities open to you as a Special Agent of the FBI. Second, I want you to get to know the men and women I interviewed, because they're the ones who are going to let you "walk in their shoes."

THE AUTHOR

Some of you might know my story already from reading Mindhunter. *But for those of you who don't, here is the condensed version.*

I grew up in Hempstead, Long Island. I never had any idea I'd become an FBI Agent; I didn't even know how to spell FBI. My big ambition was to be a veterinarian. For three summers while I was in high school, I went up to Ithaca, New York, and worked for the Cornell Extension Service. So while my buddies were out playing in the sun at Jones Beach, I was shoveling cow manure.

When it came time to apply for college, I sent off my scores and my grades to Cornell, and they wrote back a very nice letter thanking me for my interest and suggesting that maybe Cornell wasn't the right place for me. They said I might be better off at another fine academic institution: Montana State University.

5

So I packed up and headed out west to Montana, where the men are men and the sheep are nervous. I spent a few semesters there, diligently working on my extracurricular activities. When I bombed out of MSU, I went home to Long Island for a while, then joined the Air Force.

While I was in the Air Force, I finally started getting my act together. I did some volunteer work with mentally disabled kids, and found that to be tremendously rewarding. I was stationed in New Mexico then, and decided I'd get a degree in education. I started taking classes at Eastern New Mexico University, fondly referred to by its students and alumni as Enema U.

I'd met an FBI agent at the gym we both went to, and shortly after I got my degree, he suggested I apply to the Bureau. I still had no burning interest in law enforcement, but this guy seemed to be doing okay. He was making a nice salary, while I was scraping by and living in a basement apartment that was more like a glorified Roach Motel. So I applied, and I got in.

I fell in love with the work. After a few years in the Bureau, I ended up in the Behavioral Sciences unit, analyzing the "why" to develop ways of finding out the "who" behind the most brutal crimes. More and more, I kept thinking that we were missing something basic. We had all these ideas about criminal thinking, but they were really just speculation from the outside. I felt we needed to talk to the criminals themselves to get the real story. After all, they're the real experts.

Now, as you will read in Doug Rhoads's story, this was a time when the first thing a new agent was told was "Don't screw up." That fear of embarrassing the Bureau sometimes translated into a fear of trying anything new, so I had a hard time getting anyone to listen to me.

By 1978, I was giving classes with the Bureau's "road school" for police officers around the country. One day, a colleague and I were on the road in California. We had some time on our hands and I said, "Let's see if there's anyone we can talk to near here." There was: serial killer Ed Kemper.

Kemper was California's "Co-Ed Killer." Like most violent criminals, he'd had a troubled childhood. He never got along with his mother, who didn't like him because he looked like his father. His favorite game as a young child was to have his sister tie him up so he could pretend he was dying in a gas chamber. Later, he killed and mutilated the family's two cats. Finally, his mother sent him to live with his grandparents, who lived in northern California.

One day, when Ed was 14, he got irritated with his grandmother. He shot her and stabbed her over and over again with a kitchen knife. He figured his grandfather wouldn't be happy when he discovered what had happened, so Ed shot him too. Kemper told the cops, "I just wondered how it would feel to shoot Grandma." He was sent to a mental hospital, but released when he turned 21.

Kemper then went to live with his mother, who worked at the University of California at Santa Cruz. Not surprisingly, his relationship with her hadn't improved. The rage he felt toward her eventually was unleashed. Within two years, Kemper started killing again.

He quickly developed a simple but effective technique. He'd offer a ride to a young woman, kill her in the car, then take her home where he'd sexually assault the body and take photographs of it. Then he'd dump the body by the side of the road.

Kemper eventually killed six women, becoming bolder as he went along. As a condition of his release, he had to keep regular appointments with a state psychiatrist. He reported to one appointment with the head of a 15-year-old girl in the trunk of his car. That day, he was judged no longer a threat to society.

Finally, Kemper went for his real target. One Saturday night, he beat his mother to death with a hammer, decapitated the corpse and raped it. He cut out his mother's larynx and tossed it into the garbage disposal. But when he flipped the switch, the disposal threw the larynx back up at him. Kemper complained later, "Even after she was dead, she was still bitching at me. I couldn't get her to shut up."

The next morning, Kemper called a friend of his mother's and invited her over for lunch. When she arrived, he killed her and fled. Within days, he called police from the road and surrendered.

Kemper turned out to be the perfect guy to begin our interviews with. For one thing, he's very smart—brilliant, really. And he has a lot of insight into himself and his crimes. I actually like Ed. Do I think this intelligent, sensitive man should be let out of prison, under any circumstances? Hell, no. He's dangerous, and he always will be.

Interviewing Kemper confirmed my theory: The criminals themselves had a lot to teach us. We continued our interviews and, with Ann Burgess, eventually wrote *Sexual Homicide: Patterns and Motives*. A few years later, we followed up with the *Crime Classification Manual*, which was the biggest portion of my thesis for my doctoral degree.

Eventually, profiling became accepted as a legitimate investigative technique, and even as

a legal, valid way of linking violent crimes. By
the time I retired from the Bureau in 1995, the
profiling unit had contributed to the capture
and prosecution of some of the nation's most
dangerous criminals. And that's something I'll
always be proud of.

Bruce Koenig

One of the finest forensics experts I ever worked with was Bruce Koenig. Whenever we had any kind of audio problem, we knew that if anything could be done, Bruce and his people would do it. The strength of the Bureau's forensics, engineering, and other technical support departments makes a huge difference to law enforcement agencies across the country and around the world.

I'm probably not the typical FBI agent. I
never thought about being in the Bureau; I never
played G-man when I was a kid. I got my
undergraduate degrees in physics and math. While
I was in school, I worked for the Bureau of
Commercial Fisheries, feeding rats.
Incidentally, this time counted toward my federal
pension when I retired—not that I'd planned it
that way; it's just a job that came up.

I graduated during the Vietnam War era and
served in the army. I went in under the officer
candidate school, but got in and said, "Well, I
don't think this is going to be my direction, to
be a military officer for life." So I didn't go to
officer; I just became an enlisted man. I was

transferred to Fort Campbell, Kentucky, and assigned to clerk and photography duties. My wife always says they took a look at my physics degree, got as far as "P-H" and said, "Well, that must be photography."

When I was getting ready to leave the service, I started applying for jobs in the aerospace industry. Well, this was the late '60s, early '70s, when the space program was being cut back, and the aerospace industry just wasn't hiring. They were laying off guys with Ph.D.'s. Somebody I talked to said, "Oh yeah, the FBI's hiring. They want science degrees." Well, going to work for the FBI had never occurred to me. But if they were hiring, I figured why not. I applied and took a test and got in. This was in 1970.

I didn't come in thinking that the FBI would be my career. I thought I'd be in the Bureau for three years, aerospace would open up, and I'd go there. But once I got in, I changed my mind. I loved the job. I never thought about leaving until it was time for me to retire.

I didn't plan to end up in forensics. It was in the back of my mind I might be sent back to the lab. But once I got in the field, I really liked the field investigations. My first posting was in Atlanta, and then I went to Detroit.

I spent four years in the field, handling a lot of fugitive work and Selective Service violators—this was when the draft was in effect. And in Detroit, I handled extremist matters that included the Ku Klux Klan and a violent faction of the Black Panther Party. We weren't interested in the groups' ideology, just the violent actions. I very much enjoyed getting in the car, being in the street, and doing good things.

After about three years in the field, I was getting pressure to move up and become a supervisor in Detroit. I realized I'd probably be behind a desk for the rest of my career, and I wasn't sure that's what I wanted to do. Then the engineering section, which was part of the FBI Laboratory at that time, offered me a supervisor's job in Washington, DC. I thought about it and said, "Well, I think I'd rather go be a supervisor in Washington than be a supervisor in Detroit."

That was when I got into doing tape recording work. I really enjoyed it. I started publishing papers in technical journals and really pushing the envelope of where we could go. And, lo and behold, I became the Bureau's tape expert. I didn't set out to do that, but the work was so fascinating that I kept exploring what could be done with this evolving science.

Early in my career, I worked on some tape analyzing the Kennedy assassination. I was in twelfth grade when President Kennedy was assassinated, so I obviously didn't investigate the original case. I had been in the engineering section four years in 1979 when a group known as the Stokes Committee released a report on the Kennedy assassination. They had analyzed some audiotape of the event, and came out and said there was a 95 percent or greater chance that there was a second shooter from the grassy knoll.

The Department of Justice asked the FBI to look at it, and the project was assigned to me. I went through what the Stokes Committee had found and wrote up my report, which was published by the Department of Justice. Basically, I couldn't say whether they were right or wrong, but that there was no scientific support for their conclusion based on their own studies.

Then the project went over to the National Academy of Sciences, and I worked with them. They were gracious enough to actually mention my name in their report, which rarely happens.

The Stokes Committee had isolated certain sounds on the tape and identified these as gunshots from a second shooter. We were able to show conclusively that the information area they were looking at actually occurred well after the shooting. The President's limousine was already

out of Dealy Plaza on the way to the hospital.
Whatever they were pointing out as these other
shots had to be something else; the time just
didn't add up.

I noticed that the *Washington Post* put the
original story about the second shooter on the
front page. But when the National Academy report
came out, it was on the fifth page back. News
showing a story was wrong doesn't sell papers.
Every paper in the country did the same thing. I
still run into people who talk about that
second-shooter report; they never heard that it
has been proven wrong.

There was one interesting sidelight to that
case. Earlier, I'd worked on a shooting down in
Greensboro, North Carolina, involving the Ku
Klux Klan and the Socialist Workers Party. There
had been a march, and the two groups were across
the street from one another. Shooting broke
out—several of the Socialist Workers group were
injured, and five or six were killed. The Klan
was accused of opening fire on the SWP, who said
that they had not fired back.

I did a big gunshot analysis, and I was able
to show that both sides fired approximately the
same amount of shots. I was able to take the
echoes off the buildings and actually pinpoint,
usually within two or three feet, where each
shot originated. If you look at the videos, you

rarely see anyone firing. Someone in one group would shoot, the cameras would swing over to that side of the street, and they'd stop firing. And then the other side would fire, so the cameras would swing back. You only saw a handful of people actually firing. But based on analysis of the audio, often you could match up the source of a gunshot and the shooter, based on the person's position in the crowd.

Anyway, when I was working on the Kennedy case, I noticed that one of the waveforms from that audio looked exactly like one of the waveforms from the Greensboro case. We put it in our report just to show that by itself, this kind of waveform analysis isn't very conclusive.

When I retired, I was the project manager of the audio-videotape division, which is fairly high up. But I was pretty good at getting the paperwork out of the way, so I was keeping the administrative tasks down to 30 or 40 percent of my time.

The rest I spent in the lab. I like doing things. Hands on. And when you're in management, if you try to push too hard, you can actually mess everything up. And so I avoided that step. If I hadn't retired, they probably would have made me a unit chief. I don't think there had been much doubt about that Rather than end my career pushing paper, I retired and opened up a consulting business. I still spend two or three days a week working at the Bureau. I still do most of their complex audio cases.

There's such a range of what you can do with tape. First, you can enhance it, make it more understandable. That's probably the easiest exam in the tape group, and the biggest bargain. When I left, I'd guess audio enhancement was about 60 or 70 percent of the work. Voice comparisons was an evolving field. It's not conclusive as a means of identification, but it's a systematic way of comparing voices.

I spent most of my career and I still spend most of my time now doing authentication— determining whether or not a tape has been altered or not, whether or not it is original. Authentication is a complex area; it usually takes about five to ten years work in the field to start really being comfortable with it.

I also do some signal analysis. Signal analysis means looking at general wave nonvoice signals. The simplest thing would be deciphering touch-tones. You hear a series of touch-tone beeps on a recording and you figure out what the number is. The harder parts are things like gunshot analysis—how many shots were fired, or whether they are gunshots.

I remember we worked on one case where a guy got hit over the head with a baseball bat. The sound of the impact was recorded on a 911 call, and a bat was found on the scene. We had to determine, by the sound, whether that bat could have been the weapon. And the bat matched.

That's one of the things I love about this work. You never know what's coming up next.

Phil Grivas

Phil is the kind of guy you always hope is going to run any organization. He's smart, he's hard-working, and most important, he never forgets what it was like to be one of the troops. Phil's now enjoying a well-deserved life of leisure with his wife.

I was born and raised in New York City. I attended local schools in Manhattan. And then at the age of 14, we moved to Queens, and I attended a local high school there. I graduated in January of 1963. And then from '63 to '64, I worked in a large office in Manhattan, in the mail room. In 1964, I joined the United States Army and served there for two years. I was discharged in the March of 1966. And then I was appointed to the New York City Police Department on August 1, 1966.

I'd planned on becoming a police officer ever since I was a very, very young fellow. I grew up without a father. My parents were divorced, and for a great deal of time it was just me, my mother, and my sister.

All through my childhood, the policeman on the corner, the neighborhood beat cop, always represented a kind of role model for me. A strong male figure. Everybody in the neighborhood always had a great deal of respect for him. So that's what I wanted to do when I grew up.

I was very methodical about it. In those days policemen were drafted just like anybody else was. So I knew the smart thing would be to get my military obligation out of the way before I went into the Police Academy. That's why I joined the Army.

Then while I was in the Army, I studied for the police exam and flew home to take it, about six months before I was discharged. I passed it, and so when I came out of the service, I just continued along with the rest of the process— medical tests, physical tests, psychological exams, things of that nature.

I'd researched exactly what the requirements were. And I made sure that I had everything that was required.

At that point the FBI was something totally alien to me. I first really became exposed to the Bureau after I'd been with the police force about two years.

One day I was on patrol, and a woman came running out of an apartment building and said, "Somebody's breaking into the mailboxes."

So I said, "Okay, stay outside." I walked in with my partner, and sure enough, there was a junkie, trying to pry open the mailbox, to get Social Security checks, whatever. We grabbed him and brought him back to the station house.

Breaking into a mailbox, that's a federal offense. The Postal Inspector came, took the prisoner. I gave the Inspector a statement. Then I was subpoenaed to federal court, to testify against this man.

While I was in court, and waiting to be called, I struck up a conversation with the man sitting next to me, who happened to be an FBI agent. I don't know his name. I don't even remember what he looked like. But we talked for about a half hour. And I asked him a lot of questions about the FBI. And I was just so impressed by his answers, how he presented himself, how he presented the Bureau. I was really taken by it.

The next time I was downtown, I stopped off at the New York office of the FBI. And I'm at the reception desk, and I said, "My name's Philip Grivas, I'm a police officer, and I'd be interested in what the qualifications are to be an agent."

"Oh, sure, just have a seat."

An agent came out to meet me, and the first thing he said was, "What is your degree in?"

And I said, "Degree? I don't have a degree."

The guy looked at me like I fell off a truck. And he says, "Well, look. You have to have a minimum four-year college degree before you can even be considered for a position with the FBI. And then you need a couple years of investigative experience, and this and that."

I said, "Okay, thank you very much."

I went home, and I spoke to my wife about it, and started getting geared up for this new goal.

The next month I signed up for classes at the John Jay College of Criminal Justice, and graduated in three-and-a-half years, still working full time as a policeman. At one point, I took 50 credits in one year—21 credits in one semester, eight over the summer, and 21 again in the fall. It just seemed like every week that went by, I just got more and more drawn to this idea, becoming an FBI agent.

My wife was very supportive, and so were my friends. They all said, "Well, Phil, this is what you wanna do, good luck." But there was no guarantee that after I completed my degree, that I would even be granted an interview. Then there was the oral exam, the written exam, the background check. But I just had to give it a shot.

My wife had been working at a bank, and the last year I was in school she got tired of it,

and was kind of undecided where she wanted to go.
So I said, "Well, why don't you apply for the
Bureau? Maybe they'll have some administrative
assignment there."

She said, "Well, why not?" She applied, and
she was accepted. She became a clerical employee
in the New York office.

Now, she was kind of cute. *More* than kind of.
And she still is. So they put her at the
reception desk. The Assistant Director in Charge
of the New York office, Mr. Malone, had his
office on the same floor. Every so often, he'd be
in the reception area, waiting for the elevator
or something, and he'd just engage her in
conversation.

One day he noticed she had a little miniature
version of my shield on her sweater. Malone
recognized it, and said, "Whose policeman's
badge is that?"

She said, "Oh, that's my husband's. He's a
policeman up in the Bronx. He's going to school
now. He's interested in applying to the Bureau."

So he says to her, "He is? Well, when he's
ready to graduate, you let me know."

As far as I'm concerned, this was like
winning the Lotto.

When I was a couple of weeks away from
graduating, Malone stopped by her desk again,
and said, "Well, how's your husband doing?"

"Oh, he's doing very well. He graduates in a couple weeks."

"Really? Did he get his application in?"

"Yes, he did."

"Okay. Have him see me Monday morning."

She comes home, and she tells me this. My heart almost stopped.

I call up one of my close friends, and we sat down. I said, "Look. This guy's gonna ask me questions. I wanna be prepared. I want you to throw questions at me, anything you can think of that he might ask me. I don't want to sit there— flat-footed, mouth open."

We took a long walk, for a couple of hours. And he would just shoot questions at me, quizzing me on everything from political science topics to my knowledge of current events. Law enforcement issues. Anything we could possibly think of that might come up.

And my friend says, "I've read that when they conclude an interview, they'll sometimes ask, 'Is there anything you'd like to say?' You should have something prepared for that."

So I went into the office, and I took the written examination that was issued at that time. And then I was escorted into Malone's office. Very prestigious-looking office. Huge desk, paneled walls. I was really taken by it. I was thinking, "Boy. I can't believe I got this far."

He asked me a bunch of questions about the police department, and this and that. And then he asked me, "Well, Philip. Is there anything you would like to say, before we conclude this interview?" And oh, I was really itching.

I looked at him, leaned forward, looked him in the eye, and said, "Sir, I really believe that if given the opportunity, I can make a positive contribution to the Bureau."

He leaned back, big smile. And then he said, "I believe you will, Philip. I believe you will."

I was sworn in on September 11th, 1972, and then I was transferred to St. Louis for my first office.

It was kind of a culture shock. A former New York City policeman—I had to tone myself down a little bit. Not that I was overbearing—never have been, I don't think. It's just that New York City, the Bronx, is a very different place from St. Louis, and the work of a policeman is very, very different from the work of an FBI agent.

When you're a cop, you're in uniform. Often you're patrolling in a high-crime neighborhood, and you're driving around, or you're walking around. You've got your eyes going all over the place. You're very aware of your surroundings.

Anything can happen at any time. And when you're
out there in uniform, you're it. And all eyes are
on you. You're expected to respond immediately.
As an FBI agent, you're more like a detective.
You go to the scene *after* the crime has been
committed. There isn't the same type of
tenseness and stress associated with the job.

So in St. Louis, that was when I first found
out I had to pull back a little bit. Relax a
little bit. Just take things a little bit slower.
Learn the administrative requirements, as well as
the practical investigator procedures. It just
took a little time, like when you start out in
any job. I did have a big leg up, having the
experience that I did, dealing with certain
elements and handling myself on the street. That
was a plus, a *big* plus.

We started out working in applicant matters
and general criminal matters. I found myself
being very attracted to fugitive cases, and I
ended up working mostly fugitives while I was
there. I was just better suited to going after
those kinds of people, rather than people who
were committing white-collar crimes—bank fraud,
embezzlement crimes, organized crime cases, loan
sharking, things like that. Fugitives are
individuals that commit felony violations,
mostly violent crimes. They've been identified
by the local authorities, and warrants have been

issued, and they've fled the jurisdiction in order to avoid prosecution.

From the beginning, I've wanted to catch the bad guys. And these, to me, were the bad guys, and the people who were doing the most harm to people. I've always been more comfortable on the street, dealing with certain people, a certain element. There's the physicalness of it. When you're dealing with certain people, they respect strength. And they respect people that know how to act, and stand up.

I never did, nor will I ever, take anything away from the guys or the gals who handle surveillance work, or espionage work, or organized crime, or white-collar crime. Those crimes are out there and they need to be dealt with. But early on, I learned that I was drawn to the more active, more physical aspects of the job.

So I was in St. Louis for three and a half years. I was transferred back to New York in July of 1976. I stayed there for 20 years. Finished out my career there—I retired in 1996.

When I first got back, I was assigned to the the Weathermen Fugitive Squad. The Weathermen were responsible for a lot of violent, criminal behavior during the Vietnam War era. They had a hand in a bombing at the University of Wisconsin in Madison—the math building was bombed, and one person was killed.

So for a couple of months, I was on that squad, helping track some of these people who'd fled prosecution. And then I was assigned to the bank robbery squad. I worked the bank robberies for five years, and then transferred to the fugitive squad for about five or six years.

In 1987, I was promoted to supervisor, and I was made the special assistant to the Assistant Director in charge of the New York office. I remained in that capacity from 1987 to 1994. And then the last few years I was in the Bureau, I was the supervisor in charge of the Operations Center in the New York office.

I really enjoyed working fugitives and bank robberies. I got a great deal of professional and personal satisfaction out of that. But I think there's a natural progression in a lot of people's careers. You get to a particular point in time, you say, "You know what? I think it's time to do something else." That was when I was approached by the Assistant Director in charge of the office, who asked me if I'd be interested in coming up and working with him.

I'd never thought about it before, going up the administrative ladder. But gee, when you get an offer from the number-one guy in the office— I've got to be honest, it's very flattering. I mean, there are 1,100 agents in the office. To be asked to do something like that was something special to me.

That was a big change. You have more responsibilities as a supervisor. You don't just have your own cases—you have everybody, and their cases. And if you're the kind of individual who's conscientious about your work, and take a good deal of pride in it, you'll have a lot of problems with people who don't have the same work ethic. So, you adjust, as all new supervisors do. First thing you learn is, you can't expect everybody to work at your standard. But there should be a minimum standard that you, as a supervisor, can be happy with.

I had other positions, too. I was the commanding officer of the SWAT team, and I was also the agent in charge of the hostage negotiation team. And for 17 years I was in charge of the security detail responsible for escorting the last five U.S. attorneys general whenever they were in New York, *and* the last three FBI Directors when they were in the city.

The first time I was asked to do it, I was in the bank robbery squad—William Webster had just become FBI Director at the time. The ADC called me in the office and said, "Phil, the Director is coming in tomorrow and I want you to pick him up and escort him and stay with him and make sure he gets in and out all right."

Well, I went home and I told my wife, "Honey, you're not gonna believe this. All these agents in New York and the boss asked *me*." And then it dawns on me—if anything happened to this guy, it'd be on my head. *Lots* of pressure. It's kind of a Catch-22 situation. If you do a good job, which takes a tremendous amount of work, you're always gonna be asked to do it again. If you do a lousy job, well, not only are you not gonna be asked again, but you could get fired. When I'd recruit people to work with me on the detail, I'd say, "Look. I was selected and I am selecting you. And this is completely voluntarily. These people, they're very high profile. They're very, very important. If anything ever happens to them, you can't imagine the pressure we're going to be placed under. So, let's do a good job. Let's be professional. Let's keep our heads up. But you'll go places. Accompanying these people, you'll do things and see things that you'll never have the opportunity to see or do without them."

Of course, handling both the AG and the Director, it got hectic sometimes. I'd be at home and get a call: "Phil, the Attorney General is coming in with an entourage and they're

spending the weekend in New York. Handle
everything."

I had to make hotel reservations, get guys
lined up to handle the escort, contact the
airports, go over their complete itinerary, send
advance teams out. This is all on top of my
normal responsibilities at work. Then the
Director would come in the next week, and I'd get
to do it all over again. That took an enormous
toll over the years.

Sometimes what drove me nuts wasn't so much
the possibility of a dedicated terrorist effort.
If that were the case, not only would the AG or
the Director be dead, but I'd be dead, too. But
trying to prepare for and deal with the normal
stuff that happens in New York City—that was
what really got to me. The crazy cab driver, the
guy running out of a store firing a gun. Any of
the things that can happen on any day in a city
of eight million people.

Still, it's a kick, in a way. "Wow! These
people must think I know what the hell I'm
doin'!" And I'm honored. But boy, it doesn't
come without a price. A lot of sleepless nights.
A lot of, "Did I do this? Did I check that right?
Did we plan for that?" And we were the people
they relied on for *everything*. "I forgot to pack
my tux shirt. I need a shirt for my tuxedo." They
come in and it's a crazy, wild town: "Phil, can

we do that? Phil, can we do that?" And your planning goes out the window.

When you're doing this for a long period of time with people, you develop a rapport with them. I mean, they're still the Attorney General, the FBI Director, and you're still just Agent Phil Grivas. But when you see them for the twentieth time that year, it's "Hey, how's your son, Phil?"

And you become privy to a lot of information. I made it real clear to my guys and my gals that we would *never* repeat anything outside of our own circle. That was just one of the ground rules. You're around these people so much and you literally have to stand close to them all the time. You can't protect somebody from across the room. The trick was trying to stand close to these people without them noticing you or feeling you. So you're standing there with a little earpiece in your ear and people staring at you, eating hors d'oeuvres, drinking wine. And they're in tuxes and you're in a dark suit.

I was so grateful when I left and I looked back and said, "I can't believe it. Nothing happened. Seventeen years I did that and I never had a negative experience." Same with the SWAT team. Never had an injury on my team, in all those years. I was so grateful.

Bob McGonigel

Bob was my very first partner out of the Academy. There we were, on the streets of Detroit, looking at each other and saying, "What the hell are we supposed to do now?" Well, we figured it out. Bob was a terrific partner—focused and no-nonsense when that's what the job called for, but a guy with a great sense of humor, too. He stayed on the streets all of his career, doing some really top-level organized crime work. Agents like Bob are the backbone of the Bureau. He and his wife are now living in Oregon, a place that Bob assures me has the best weather in the country—he did the research on it.

I'm a native of northern New Jersey, and while I was in high school, I worked after school in a law firm, because I wanted to be an attorney. My dad was a police officer and worked closely with the Bureau on a lot of cases. He knew it was possible to work for the FBI in a clerical capacity, attend school, and graduate. If the FBI felt you were qualified, they might hire you as an agent.

I wasn't really completely set on becoming an agent at that point, but I knew I had to pay my own way through college, and that seemed like a pretty good way to do it. So I went to work for the Bureau in the Newark Field Office in July 1962. While I worked there, I went to Rutgers and got a degree in history. I felt that was a good preparation for law school, which was what I still had in mind as an option. There was no guarantee I'd be hired as an Agent, and being an attorney would be a good fallback.

But having worked in that law office, I saw that although being a lawyer looked like a lovely career, it could be rather mundane and boring. The FBI didn't seem like that at all—no two days would be the same. And I was right. I was really able to observe what the agents did. It got to the point where becoming an Agent interested me so much, I forgot all about the pursuit of a law degree.

Those first years at the FBI, I was a combination security guard, teletype operator, radio dispatcher, file clerk, and complaint taker from the public. I got to see how everything worked from all different angles. That was a great education, a great opportunity. And there were a lot of young men and women who worked there while they went to college. It wasn't an official program—there was nothing laid out and there was no guarantee that you would become an agent. As a matter of fact, at certain field offices around the country, being a clerk lessened your opportunities to be an agent. The Special Agent in Charge at Newark the whole time I was a clerk didn't like people going that route.

But I made it anyway. I was sworn in as a Special Agent on September 25, 1971. My first posting was Detroit, Michigan. In training school, I'd guessed that I'd be assigned there.

We had a pool based on where we all thought we'd be sent, and I won the pool. I just had a feeling.

Detroit was a good town to learn the business of law enforcement. I was rather liberal in college. I was naive, as most young people are about the world. When you're in law enforcement, you're out there trying to do a good job, trying to right the wrongs. You think of yourself as being on the side of right, so of course people are going to help you out. Then you go out in the field and realize that no, people aren't necessarily going to cooperate with you. Lots of doors are slammed in your face, and lots of calls are not returned. Kind of shocking. But you have to adjust quickly if you're going to survive.

You develop persistence, get an insight for human behavior. And you do it fast. At the time I was there, the Detroit office had an awful lot of new agents, and not many seasoned agents to teach you the ropes. Many, many times John and I would go out into the field and discuss what we were going to do before we actually did it. "All right, how does this sound? Okay, and then you'll do that, okay?" We'd pretty much proceed on a lot of common sense, and on a little bit of the manual of rules and regulations. All our cases were reviewed by a supervisor. But we planned our own day-to-day activities.

When John and I first got to Detroit, there was a very large raid directed at members of organized crime: bookies and betting and so forth. But at that point, I didn't do much with organized crime. Like most young agents just starting out, I worked pretty much general criminal cases: bank robberies, fugitives, thefts, interstate shipment of stolen goods (which were largely tractor-trailers), and things like that. Vietnam was still going on, so we handled deserters and draft dodgers. That actually provided us with an excellent opportunity to do the basic things that law enforcers do. You just had the warrant, and you went out and got the body. We got to make a lot of arrests. There was lots of hands-on experience, going out and doing it, doing the investigation, doing the footwork.

I was in Detroit for a little bit over a year. For my good work, I was rewarded with a transfer to Cleveland, Ohio. Cleveland was a lot like Detroit, only a little smaller.

I was in Cleveland for about two years, until February of 1974. Then I got a transfer to New York City. No one wanted to go to New York, but I'd requested it. I liked Cleveland, but I didn't want to spend the rest of my life there. I wanted to move on in my career, and pursue something else, somewhere else.

My tour in New York began the day that Patty
Hearst was kidnapped. I spent a little over
three years there, then I requested a transfer
to Newark, New Jersey. I got that one, too. The
Bureau's transfer policy was loosening up, and
it was easier to move around—particularly if
you asked to go to what the pool of agents
considered to be an undesirable place. And
Newark is considered an undesirable place by a
lot of people. The majority of people. Can't
imagine why.

I worked in Newark until January of 1981,
when I went to Atlantic City. In October 1983, I
went back to Newark. I'd been stricken with
colon and bladder cancer, and I wanted to be
nearer the hospitals in New York City. Then in
May 1989, I went back to New York, and finished
out my career there.

That's sort of the thumbnail sketch of my
career. All along, I traveled to other divisions
to work on particular cases, for a month, two
months, six months at a time. I went to St. Louis
on a terrorist case for a couple of months. I
went to Miami on an organized crime case for a
couple months; and I went to Buffalo on another
organized crime case.

Early on, I started developing a lot of
experience on organized crime cases. Growing up
in Newark, there were many organized crime

figures in my neighborhood. And, of course, my father was a policeman, so organized crime was something familiar from a very early age.

I'd go in, help set up surveillance of suspects, interview suspects, help analyze the material, determine promising suspects, promising leads. I enjoyed that organized crime traveling work, and I did a lot of it, but I'm really a jack-of-all-trades. If you name a violation of law, somewhere or other in my career, I've worked on it. And that's exactly what I wanted. When I was a clerical employee, I always was frustrated by the fact that I wasn't out of the office doing these things. I was reading about it. I was hearing about it. But I wasn't doing it. And that's why I never really was interested in advancing to the supervisory level in the FBI. Because I didn't want to read about it, and I didn't want to hear about it. I had already done that for enough years!

One of the worst cases I worked on was a bombing at LaGuardia Airport in the '70s. I'd certainly seen corpses before, but that was the first time I'd seen such devastation. The smell of death hanging in the air.

I was home at the time. It was about 7 P.M. I was in graduate school back then, and I was working on a term paper. I received a phone call, and it's the office. There's been a bombing at

LaGuardia, several people killed. There'd been an agent injured. He was an out-of-towner, coming into the New York office, and he just happened to be walking by the site.

I wasn't a bomb expert, but I was on a squad that had investigated several bombings and bomb scares in the city. At that stage, I was just helping at the crime scene bysifting through the rubble and gathering evidence.

I have to say, I was very impressed with the New York City Police Bomb Squad. They are a fine bunch of professionals—I was really impressed with their skill. I also worked with their arson-explosion squad on the subsequent investigation. It was a great experience for me. You always hear about rivalries between different agencies and departments. That's true, there are some petty jealousies, but when a major case occurs, the line people really come together because their only goal is solving the case.

JIM MCFALL

Jim's forgotten more than I ever knew about firearms and weaponry. I first got to know him when we were both teaching at the National Academy, and I've always had a tremendous amount of respect for him. He's now the Executive Director of the Society of Former Special Agents.

My interest in the FBI came about in 1964 when I'd returned from service in the navy. I'd gone back to my old company and was working at my old job. I was generally happy doing what I was doing but I was also a little bit bored. I was a licensee engineer for an electronics manufacturing company in Philadelphia, and I handled the overseas licensees. It was a good job, a great company, a great boss, but something was missing. I'd been a naval intelligence officer during the Cuban Missile Crisis, and civilian life didn't have the same flavor as it did when I was in the navy.

So I started looking around, casually, and one of my friends mentioned that the FBI was hiring. I wasn't a lawyer or an accountant, but I thought I'd make an inquiry anyway. I just walked into the Philadelphia office of the FBI and was introduced to an agent. I gave him my background and we had a great conversation. We hit it off right away. He said that I was eligible to apply under the modified program, which I did.

I was accepted, and entered the new agent class that started training on January 25, 1965.

My first posting was Atlanta, Georgia. Reported there on May 1, 1965. For the most part new agents did background investigations on applicants, a process that we'd just been through ourselves, and we handled "car cases"— interstate transport of motor vehicles. We learned how to inspect and search recovered stolen vehicles for evidentiary material, and conduct an investigation to find the person who transported the car. And then gradually we'd be assigned more and more complicated cases.

In July of 1965, there was a great deal of civil rights activity in Georgia and in all the Southern states. I was sent on a series of special assignments to investigate violations of the federal civil rights law. Some of those assignments would last two or three days, or they might last two weeks, until the case was fleshed out. Then I'd go back to Atlanta.

Generally there'd be a team of FBI agents and whenever possible we'd cooperate with the local officers. In some areas—not all, but some—we encountered great hostility. On more than one occasion, I've gone nose-to-nose with deputies and sheriffs and ranking officers in police departments and told them flat out that they were dangerously close to obstruction of justice and interfering with a federal officer in the performance of his duty. Not a threat—a statement of law, a statement of fact. If they persisted in hindering our investigation they could face federal charges. For the most part they'd back off, and we'd go on with our jobs.

You have to appreciate the time and the location. We're talking about the mid-'60s, the deep South, generally the most rural parts. There were police officers and deputy sheriffs who were as upset as we were about some of the violations that were being committed. But these officers in these local areas knew these people committing the violations. They had a certain conflict, as it were, in their role as a law enforcement officer, and their role as a friend, a neighbor, a relative.

Being from the North, I got my share of comments. One gentleman made a lot of disparaging remarks about the FBI and "damn Yankees." He finally said to me, "If you think it's so bad down here, why'd you come?" I looked at him and I said, "Mr. Hoover made me."

And that was the truth of it. I was under orders to come down and investigate violations of federal law. And in some places, things were so bad I saw violations occur right in front of me.

I saw one young fellow in a town called
Newton, Georgia. He was leading a group down a
sidewalk around the Baker County courthouse.
There were maybe 15 people in the group, and this
young fellow, about 19 or 20 years of age, this
young fellow was carrying a sign calling for
equal rights and the right to register to vote.
Of course there was a crowd of locals watching.
One of them broke out of the group across the
street and ran over and hit this kid right in the
back of the head with a maul handle. This is like
an ax handle, only round. A real weapon, a club.
The kid did a flip in the air, actually did a
flip, and landed flat on his back. Just lay
there. I was sure he was dead. Then the guy who
hit him turned around and ran away.

In a situation like that, you're torn
between two things. One, render aid to the
victim, and two, catch the guy who did it. I
rendered aid to the victim first. Then we got
some help and went looking for the guy who hit
him. Well, he lost himself in the crowd. All the
rednecks would stand shoulder to shoulder so you
couldn't get through. They wouldn't grab you—
they knew better than that—but they'd just keep
stepping in front of you.

It took us a few days, but we identified the
assailant. We just kept talking to people, going
back and asking questions over and over again.

41

You can't let go and you can't ignore it. If you ignore it, they'll do it again.

I went all over Georgia on civil rights cases. It culminated in July 1965, when I was assigned to a Bureau Special. That means a team of agents on a particularly sensitive assignment, under the supervision of an Inspector from the Bureau headquarters. I ended up on a roving team: We went to Natchez, Mississippi, and worked on Klan cases there, especially the Silver Dollar group. These were dedicated Klansmen with a propensity for violence. Then the team moved over into Louisiana, working with resident agencies under the New Orleans Field Office to assist them in intensifying the investigation of the Klan in those areas.

I was in the Resident Agency from April 1, 1967 to April 1, 1971, and then I was in the New Orleans Field Office, assigned to various squads. I became the bank robbery fugitive coordinator, then supervisor of the bank robbery squad, then supervisor of the white-collar crime squad and the political corruption squad.

With the fugitive investigations, we used to feel that New Orleans was a prime location to find fugitives because it's a playground. The fugitives, especially in the wintertime, would come South and go to New Orleans to play and we'd

find them. They had the Jefferson Casino in
Jefferson Parish, and they had gambling over in
Algiers, which is a section of New Orleans. It
was a party town for the bad guys.

Later on, when I was in the white-collar
crime-political corruption squad, we had a
saying that Louisiana is the only state in the
union where the citizens do not tolerate bad
government—they *demand* it. There was one old
politician there, years ago, O.K. Allen. His
claim to fame is he built a bridge to nowhere—
from nowhere, to nowhere. It's called the
Sunshine Bridge, and when it was built there was
no road leading to it, no road leading away from
it. But O.K. Allen wanted a big bridge built in
that parish and they built it. Later on they did
build roads to it, but for years it just stood
there.

In 1979 I was transferred to the FBI Academy
as a staff instructor, and I remained there until
I retired. I taught a wide gamut of students. New
agents, of course, and in-service agents who came
back. I taught police officers who were attending
the FBI National Academy, which is a graduate
school for police officers. Foreign police
officers would also send visitors in.

After I retired, I went back to the Bureau to
do a lecture for police officials in Kazakstan.
I had a very good time working with them, and was

offered a job at their training academy in
Almonte, Kazakstan. The guy who offered me the
job is the deputy chief of their police
department—it's called the PMD, I think. I
forget what the initials stand for. I have still
have the guy's business card, but it's in
Cyrillic. Anyway, I said I would think about it,
then I talked to another guy on the staff who had
been to Kazakstan, and he said, "Mac, trust me.
You *don't* want to go." So I declined. They were
good people, though.

That was one of the things I truly enjoyed
about the Academy—I had a wide variety of people
to talk to, to work with. I was in the firearms
training unit; I'm an expert firearms instructor,
and for several years I was the Bureau's expert
on less-than-lethal weapons and chemical agents.
As a matter of fact, I introduced oleoresin
capsaicin, or pepper spray, to the Bureau. I got
it from a company in Florida who sent me samples
and said "This stuff is better than sliced bread
and vanilla ice cream. Try it out." I tried it out
and, man, it'll knock your socks off.

All those years on the fugitive and bank
robbery squads, all the armed-and-dangerous
apprehensions I've been involved in, I was never
shot, never hit. *That* happened at the Academy. I
was teaching on the range and got hit by a
ricocheting round. That was three days before I

retired. A round came off a steel target, hit me right in the face, sliced through my lip and lodged in my upper gum. I had to go to the hospital and have it dug out. At my retirement party I had a great big swollen lip and a black eye from the impact.

The Bureau really puts a focus on training. What you do in training is what you'll do on the street. If you hesitate when you should react, you're going to get hurt. You might get killed. You might get other people killed. I've been away from the Academy for several years now, but I know they're constantly upgrading the training they offer so it correctly reflects the current laws, the current social situations. The Academy really makes an effort to put the agents through scenarios that are essentially the same as what they'll face in real life.

Of course, that's not always possible. Laws change, society changes. And no matter how hard you try, training isn't going to be exactly like real life. I remember I was teaching one new agents' class and I told a war story to make a point. One of the trainees took exception to the technique I employed in the story. That trainee wrote a letter of complaint to the Assistant Director of the Training Division. I got called in and was asked to explain. I said, "What do you mean, explain?"

"Well, you told these agents that you did thus and so, blah blah blah."

I said, "There's no problem with that, is there?"

"Yeah, there's a problem."

"Well, I don't know what it could be; I didn't lie."

The guy said, "You *did* that?"

"Yeah, I did."

"You can't do that!"

I just said, "You can't do it *now*. But at the time I did it, it wasn't illegal. And I made that clear to the class—the difference between the situation then and the situation now."

I don't want to go into detail—let's just say it was an aggressive way of handling a situation. What I did was perfectly within the law. People who have never been there and never handled such a situation might find it surprising, they might even find it alarming, but that's the reality of it. You've got to be prepared to handle the situation—within legal limits, but sometimes forcefully.

Sometimes I wonder if that trainee ever reached a moment in his career and thought, "*Now* I see McFall's point."

Doug Rhoads

Doug was a fine agent, someone I wish I'd had a chance to work with directly. Doug designed the FBI's recruiting program. I knew him by reputation, and I would run into him at the Academy. And every once in a while, when I was watching a college football game on TV, they would show one of the refs and I'd say, "I'll be damned—that's Doug Rhoads!" Doug has been an NCAA referee for over 20 years. Since retiring from the Bureau in 1994, Doug has worked as chief for a county sheriff's office in Virginia.

I grew up in Miami, Florida, attended public high school there. At that time Miami was more of a sleepy southern town than the big, cosmopolitan area it is now. I was born in 1944, so I'm talking about 1950, '51, '52. I was always interested in law enforcement, and we had a neighbor who worked for the FBI. He had the whole white shirt, button-down collar, snap-brim hat look, and I was impressed. Then when I was in eighth or ninth grade, we went up to DC and took the tour of the FBI headquarters. That was when I made my mind up that if I was going to be in law enforcement, I wanted to be on a national level.

I went on to undergraduate school at the University of Florida, in Gainesville. In those days there was a perception, mostly accurate, that the Bureau recruited only lawyers and accountants. I graduated in 1966, during the Vietnam era. I had taken an ROTC commission, but got a deferment to go to law school. Of course, the only reason I wanted to go to law school was because I figured that would make it easier to get into the FBI.

Then I decided, "No, I'll take my commission, get that out of the way." So I went into the military, and went to Vietnam. I got out in 1969, as a captain, and re-enrolled in law school. It was just a means to an end.

But pretty soon I realized that the FBI had expanded its modified entry program—meaning modified from law and accounting. Now, the Bureau would accept three years' work experience in a field it was interested in. Well, I had three years as an officer in the military, so I applied through the Miami Field Office, and joined the Bureau in October 1969.

That was really a heavy hiring period. The Bureau's jurisdiction was expanding—there was the Safe Streets and Crime Control Act in 1968 and the Omnibus Crime Control Act in 1970, and the Bureau needed people on the streets. The Bureau probably hired 2,000 new agents from 1970 to 1972. With all that growth, there was a new agent class every two weeks, with 52 agents each class. It was almost an assembly line.

But to be honest, given the times, given the rapid growth, given all that was there, the Bureau did like always: It rallied and did a good job. It got people through and got 'em out. When you graduated, they pretty much just gave you six bullets and said, "Get out of town, and don't get into trouble before you get where you're going."

I remember tearing open the envelope and reading "Dallas, Texas." I'm thinking, "Man, I'm from Miami, I've been to Vietnam, I'm here in Washington, I've been around a little, traveled some, but I've never been to Texas in my life." I figured at least I'd see a new place. I was married then—no children—so my wife and I headed off to Dallas. It was the best thing that ever happened to me.

I was placed on a fugitive squad with a total of eight agents. Half of them were veterans, half of them were new guys like me. You got paired up and went out and learned how to do the job. I can tell you every arrest I was in on, and about every guy on that squad. I loved every minute of it. This was something I'd wanted since I was 14 years old. I was almost like a little kid. "I don't want everyone to know how much I really like it, so I'm going to bitch about things like everybody else—but I really like it."

After I'd been there about eight months, there was an opening in a Resident Agency in Lubbock. What a place. You could roll a bowling ball from Lubbock and it'd go all the way to Minnesota. I remember snow with dirt in it, and thenthirty consecutive days with the temperature over a hundred degrees. But you know what? The way people in Texas treat law enforcement, you felt like a million bucks.

West Texas was a great place to be. The weather might have been a little weird, but the people were good. And because the RA was so small, I handled everything. They say, "These five counties are yours." You look at the map and you say, "Garza County? Where the hell is that?" So you drive down to Garza County and you walk in and say "Agent Rhoads, FBI, I'd like to meet the sheriff." You sit down and talk to them, you go to lunch with them, you share information with them, you develop a relationship with them, then you go down to Snyder and you do the same thing.

I was in Lubbock for just about 11 months. Then in March of '71, I tear the old envelope open and it says, "You're going to Richmond, Virginia." I get a phone call about five days later, it's the Special Agent in Charge in Richmond. He'd been the assistant to the Special Agent in charge in Dallas, so he knew me. He said, "Hey, I got a couple of RA openings, one in Charlottesville and the other in Roanoke. I want a guy who's experienced in an RA. What do you think about either of those two?" I said, "I'll take Charlottesville." That was it—very casual, almost conversational. So we packed up and drove

1,700 miles from Lubbock, Texas, to
Charlottesville, Virginia.

Talk about a bird's nest on the ground. There
were two veteran agents there, very distinctly
different personalities. One was a former police
officer from upstate New York, just an affable,
friendly, hardworking, easygoing guy. The second
one was an Irish Catholic from Boston with previous
navy experience. I'll never forget calling him on
the phone: "Hello, this is Doug Rhoads, I'm the new
agent, I'm here in town and I need directions." He
was telling me how to get to the office and he kept
saying, "You go down Mockit Street." Well, I can't
find this Mockit Street, so I finally say, "Is that
'M-o-c-k-i-t?' " Well, no. He's saying *Market*
Street with this thick Boston accent. I imagine he
took some getting used to for those Virginians.

Both those guys were just great mentors. I
don't think they even realized they were being
mentors to me. It was like, "Hey, here's the
third guy on the team." And we worked that way
together—very informal, loosely structured. But
when something had to be done, everybody went.
When the major surveillance happened, everybody
did it. When the big fugitive lead came in,
everybody participated.

That's where I really developed the love of
the Resident Agency. I enjoyed working with all
the different divisions of local law

enforcement. You have to rely on the state and local police a lot more when there's only three of you and you're covering 12, 13 counties. I met some great folks and just loved it. I would never have left, and didn't leave until I had to.

I remained in Charlottesville from 1971 to December 1983. I eventually became the senior RA there. The senior RA when I started retired, and then we closed a small office over in Stanton and added it into Charlottesville's territory, so we were up to five agents.

In December of '83 I was transferred back to FBI Headquarters in Washington. William Webster was director then, and they'd taken a look at the staffing issues and decided they needed to diversify their work force and set up a more systematic way of recruiting. That's where it started: "Hey, design a program for us." It was fun and challenging.

So 1983 to 1985 was the research phase, and 1985 to 1990 is when it really got going as a program. Then, in 1990, there was an opening in Charlottesville for a senior resident agent. To take the job, I'd have to take a pay cut. I'd been a unit chief, and I'd go back to a street agent. It took me about 45 seconds to decide I wanted to do it. I wanted to go back to the street, back to working cases, back to being a part of a small Resident Agency.

So October 1, 1990, I finished up seven years of the executive management thing, and now I'm back making drug arrests, working bank robberies, locking up fugitives. I got right back to it: Get your car, get your gun, get your badge, get your cases. It was the best decision I ever made in my life.

Frank Watts

I joined the Bureau just about the time Frank retired, so I never got the chance to work with him. I wish I had. Agents like Frank did some important, front-line work at a time when it wasn't easy to do.

I grew up in the little town of Wiggins, Mississippi. We had maybe a thousand in population. Only two celebrities ever came out of Wiggins—that's myself and Dizzy Dean, the Hall of Fame baseball player. Growing up, I never had any idea of becoming an FBI agent. Never even thought of it. In fact, I never even knew what an FBI agent was.

Shortly after I graduated from University of Mississippi, I was working as an office manager for a utility company, United Gas Corporation in Gulfport, Mississippi. Even though gambling was completely outlawed in the state of Mississippi, there was a lot of gambling going on. And they had what they called juice joints. These places had an electromagnetic device planted underneath craps tables, and the owners used that device to determine the roll of the dice. These machines were brought in from out of state, shipped in from Chicago. So there was an interstate angle there, and the FBI had full jurisdiction.

One morning, two FBI agents came in to my office and identified themselves. They said they'd like to have somebody help them, go and gamble at one of these juice joints to gather evidentiary information for the successful prosecution. They needed someone who was a local person and had no connection with law enforcement whatsoever. So they asked me if I would volunteer. And I said, "yeah, I'd be glad to."

They gave me money, and I went to the place they pointed out. And I promptly lost it all, because I didn't know a thing about gambling. But I went there for two or three nights, and I saw exactly what they were doing, how they were operating. I was able to give them the information they needed, and then testify during the trial. It turned out to be a successful prosecution for them.

About 60 days later those same agents came by and thanked me for my help. And then they asked me, "Would you like to be an FBI agent?"

I said, "Well, I don't know anything about it. But that was fun, you know, what we did."

So I went to New Orleans, took a test, and put in my application. And I was accepted. I went to Washington and was sworn in on May 12, 1952. After that, I was assigned to Albany, New York, which was a shock for a boy from Wiggins, Mississippi. One of Hoover's policies was to send a person completely outside of their environment for their first posting. That way, he could get all his errors out of the way in a place where there were no friends, family, or any possible political influence. That first winter was rough, I have to say.

But I served there for two years, and then went to Syracuse, New York, just briefly before I was sent to New Haven, Connecticut. The FBI had a bit of a crisis there, because of the Soviet efforts to gain information regarding the nuclear subs at the Navy Yard there. There was quite a bit of Soviet activity there.

Another policy of Hoover's was that an agent did not specialize in one particular case. We had well over 100 different classifications— bank robbing, kidnapping, espionage—and any agent was expected to be able to handle any complaint that came through the door.

So I handled all kinds of cases, from the beginning to the end. But I think it's the way with most things: If you really like working on a particular thing, and really enjoy your work, naturally you do your best work. And I really liked working the espionage cases. Trying to

identify KGB agents, trying to gather
intelligence on them; it was most intriguing to
me. So I ended up doing my best work in that
area, and I began to get more and more espionage
cases. I eventually became a supervisor of that
squad.

We learned that in order for KGB agents to
come to this country, to actively participate in
gathering what they wanted, they had to have
seven years of training. Seven full years. And
each agent had to cover every angle. Number one,
his cover story. Then the mechanics of espionage:
how to operate drop boxes, how to obtain
information, how to photograph documents, how to
microdot them. That sort of thing. And also how
to live under an assumed identity, maybe even as
an American citizen. These were very intelligent,
well-trained people. And getting to the truth in
dealing with them was very difficult. But it was
the most intriguing thing of all.

I continued to work in this area until 1964. At
that point, I was sent back down South as part of
the FBI's response to the civil rights problems
there. The White Knights of the Ku Klux Klan were
really spreading havoc throughout the south, and
particularly in Mississippi.

I was proud to do that work. I was brought up
in a traditional Southern home. My family
believed in segregation, and if you even

mentioned interracial marriage or anything like
that, my dad would turn red in the face. But there
was another side to him, too. He ran a service
station, and that's where I worked after school
all the time I was growing up. During the war,
gasoline was rationed, and money was scarce. Time
after time, a poor black farmer would come in who
really needed gasoline and couldn't afford it,
and my dad would give him some out of the ration
for one of the businesses who wouldn't use its
share. Or a family would need medicine, but they
didn't have money to pay for it. Dad would call
across the street to the pharmacist and say,
"Sombody's comin' over and he needs some
medicine. Put that on my bill."

It was easy to see how hard a time the black
families in that area had, how they were
mistreated. Then, when I got into the FBI, I saw
what was really taking place: not just denying
them the right to register to vote, but killings
and lynchings and beatings. It just wasn't in my
heart to go along with anything like that.

Anyway, after that office closed down, I
stayed in the South until I retired. My wife and I
moved up here to the Ozarks, where we can just
enjoy ourselves. And to this day, I am proud of
the work I did with the Bureau.

JANET L. ENGEL

Janet was one of the first 100 women hired by the FBI. I taught the Sexual Homicide classes at the Academy while Janet was there in the late '70s. There were only about two or three women in each class at the time. Many in the Bureau questioned women's roles and competencies. Janet's story answers those questions. Janet was one of the first women to receive a Quality In-Step Increase Award for her performance and leadership of a surveillance team.

I was born in Uniondale, Long Island, and my father was Chief of Detectives at Nassau County Police Department. I graduated from college with language abilities in French and Russian, and began a law enforcement career as a police officer at Merced, California, after my tour in the United States Air Force. My father was my role model and provided great encouragement, support, and advice as I "went federal".

The Academy was an interesting experience. I had the advantage of both military and police training, but the FBI was a mix of physical, firearms, and mental challenges. I particularly remember women with packed bags leaving the Academy as I arrived. They had "washed out." Of course men did the same... but it was the women I remembered.

There were, at any one time, only about 15 or 20 women at the Academy. We were as varied in our interests and abilitites as in the manner in which we approached the FBI culture. But in many people's eyes we were just "women."If I heard one more time "how many push-ups can you do?" while selecting breakast in the cafeteria line I might have seriously developed a trauma about buttered toast.

The Bureau culture affects both men and women. But I would say this——when I was on the police force it was clear your acceptance had to do with your ability to do the job. Once you established your competency with colleagues you were rarely "tested" again. However, I found in my early Bureau experiences each time you changed squads (especially women), there was usually an undercurrent of having to prove yourself; over and over again, no matter what your "time on the job"and proven track record. And would it be politically incorrect to mention politics in the FBI? Each division had its own pecking order, and although being a women was unique, I believe both men and women were affected by this environment.

I made life-long friends at the Academy, and finally went to the field.

My first assignment was Albany, New York, and I subsequently was transferred to New York City where I retired in 2004. While in Albany, I rotated through many squads where I received a diverse background in working investigations. The one thing most Agents will agree on is that regardless which specialties you will develop later in your career, it is vital you have "time

on the street." This means you have developed
and brought prosecutable cases to the United
States Attorney's office. This is what we do.

In New York City, I was assigned to Foreign
Counter Intelligence(the Russian Squad) due to
my language ability. I was sent to the Defense
Language School in Monterey, California, to hone
my skills. I spoke fluent Russian and spent a
good deal of time in Brighton Beach (the Coney
Island area) where many emigres resided. My
fluency often resulted in slammed doors as the
emigres believed I could be KGB.

I was always interested in transitioning
back to reactive work and was finally assigned
to a surveillance squad. In a Division the size
of New York, there were about ten surveillance
squads. This was a very tight-knit group with
unpredictable hours. It was not unusual for the
team to receive a telephone call and suddenly be
on planes to work the Imelda Marcos case in
Hawaii or matters involving international
assignments in South American and the Middle
East. I was exposed to all manners of FBI
investigations through my surveillance work, and
I very much enjoyed the camaraderie.

I finally ended my career assigned to a
criminal squad working complex auto-theft rings.
The work was challenging and exciting. I sometimes
found myself on dark New York City piers meeting

with sensitively positioned informants and working closely with prosecutors. Because of the organized crime presence in these cases, there were protection details of witnesses set to testify; threat assessments involving these witnesses, and work with the United States Marshals as some of these witnesses transitioned to the federal Witness Protection Program.

My retirement after 27 years in the Bureau was only jettisoned in 2004 by an opportunity to be involved in the United Nations' Oil for Food Scandal. It is only due to my FBI experience I could avail myself of this opportunity.

An FBI career provides numerous challenges while you are on board, and represents a standard in law enforcement as you pursue other ventures. My singular goal has always been the respect of colleagues while enjoying my work. I had both.

Jim O'Connor

Jim was a member of the team who designed the training programs at the FBI Academy. He's a sharp guy, determined to keep the Bureau at the cutting edge of investigations. He was one of the early supporters of profiling, at a time when most people thought it was a lot of B.S.—and I don't mean Behavioral Science.

When I graduated from college, I was toying with the idea of going into the Marine Corps. But then I got an assistantship and went in for my master's degree in English, and I decided to go into college teaching. I took a job at what's now Gannon University—it was Gannon College then—in Erie, Pennsylvania. I taught there for three years, and decided I needed to go back for my doctorate. I started teaching part time at Hunter College, part of the City University of New York, and working on my doctorate in English at the same time.

While I was there, I started to realize that academic politics was not going to be my forte. I had met some people when I was teaching in Gannon, one individual in particular, who had gone into the FBI and said it was a great career, I'd find it interesting, and so forth. One day I was at Hunter and finished teaching a class and was really thinking about a career change. I just walked over to the FBI office over on 69th Street and asked for an application. I filled it out and then after I put it in, I decided to just go head and make a career change. I took a job with Merrill Lynch Pierce Fenner and Smith as an executive recruiter. I think I was with them about four months when the FBI called and wanted me to start going through the exams and interviews and so forth. That following June, June of 1965, I was sworn in as a new agent.

My first office was Indianapolis, Indiana. I did fugitive work, some applicant work, primarily organized crime and vice. We handled a few white-slavery cases (white slavery is the transporting of women over state lines for immoral purposes) and gambling cases there. I was in Indianapolis a little over a year, then I got transferred to Charlotte, North Carolina.

In Charlotte, I was on the road mostly. This was during the civil rights days—I worked a lot of Klan matters, school desegregation matters. Then I was transferred to the resident agency in Durham, North Carolina. There were four of us there, handling five counties. We did all the criminal security, racial matters, everything in those five counties. It was quite an eye-opening experience.

In 1968, I was transferred back to Quantico. There were eight of us selected for the Planning and Research Unit to plan the new FBI Academy, which opened in 1972. We were chosen primarily for the variety of backgrounds: firearms, defensive tactics, arrest techniques, sociology, forensics, accounting, law. I was called because of my experience in college teaching, and my area was basically communication research.

One of the first things we did was find a university for the National Academy Program to affiliate with. We ended up with the University of Virginia. That means every class at the National Academy qualifies for academic credit, some undergraduate, some graduate.

Our primary focus was training for police. All during the time we were planning, we were also teaching police community relations all over the country. And most of us were sent back to graduate school, too. So we weren't just sitting there.

In 1972 I was transferred to the Academy as a Supervisory Special Agent. I taught the education and communication arts unit: interviewing, interrogation, education. In 1974, I finished my Ph.D. at Catholic University. The next year, 1975, I was sent to the Police Staff College in Bramshill, England. This was when the FBI was really beginning to push the international aspect, and I was the first FBI representative sent to that course.

Essentially, Bramshill is the equivalent of the FBI Academy. It's where they select and train their future chief constables through

England and Wales. There were 24 of us in that
four-month course: 16 from the United Kingdom,
and eight from the rest of the world. We had
Egyptians, Danes, a Singaporean, an Australian,
a guy from Trinidad. Two Americans: a captain
from the NYPD, and myself. This was an
executive-development type class, so we talked
abut administration, managing major cases, and
that kind of thing. Not specific investigative
techniques, as much as running a department. You
were dealing with people who were expected to
move up.

It was interesting. As they say, England and
the United States are two nations separated by a
common language. And the policing system there
is significantly different from ours. But of
course there were certain things in common:
management studies, and response to things like
terrorism. We ended up having a faculty exchange
and a student exchange with Bramshill. And later
on, with the Australian police college and the
Canadian police college.

After Bramshill, I went back to the Academy
for a year, and then got transferred to the
Inspections staff, as an Inspectors Aide. I
spent roughly a year in 1976 going around the
country inspecting FBI field offices. What we're
looking for is effectiveness, efficiency, and
economy of operation. Compliance with the

attorney general's guidelines and the federal laws. You look at the entire investigation and administrative operation of a field office.

When I first joined the Bureau, these were surprise inspections. You didn't know these guys were coming, and all of sudden they arrived. When I was an inspector's aide, there was no surprise about it. They had all kinds of interrogatories that they had to prepare for us, before we arrived. Profiles, caseloads, priorities, statistical data. What was the overall budget, and how was it spent.

So we'd fly in for an inspection, and they would meet us at the airport. And then we'd go through the two most polite lies in the Bureau. The guys from the Field Office would say, "We're happy to have you here," and we'd say, "We're here to help you."

And then I got transferred back to the Academy. I was a section chief in charge of academic affairs, which is where I stayed until I retired, in 1989.

Since then, I've been head of the criminal justice program at Northern Virginia Community College. For three years, Northern Virginia shared me with George Mason University, and I was the head of the program there.

I still go back to the Academy, as a student. I try to stay current with what's going on. You

can't ever decide you've learned all you're
going to learn; you've got to keep an open mind
to what's happening. Nothing stays the same for
long. Not even the law. Every term the Supreme
Court comes down with new decisions, and you
better be up on those decisions and know what
they mean in terms of the rules and procedures
for law enforcement.

I think we're seeing more and more
breakthroughs in other areas, too. Behavioral
sciences, forensic sciences. It's almost
staggering once you start thinking about it: DNA
analysis, all the things that are being done
today that couldn't be done just a few years ago.
You've just got to keep up, if you're going to do
any good at all.

RODNEY M. DAVIS

Rodney came to the FBI in 1967 as a clerk and in 1972 as an Agent. During those years it was not unusual for many to take this career track. Rodney was also from New York City, and was one of the first 100 African Anerican agents hired by the FBI. He had some very interesting experiences working with Extremist Groups, and has a unique story to share.

I was born and raised in Brooklyn and was first introduced to the FBI through one of those high school Career Days. I knew of the FBI but had never considered it a career option until meeting Special Agent Art Hendricks. I was aware one could apply for an Agent's position through the clerical career path. I took the test and entered on duty as a clerical staff in 1967. I finished college and took the Agent's entrance exam in 1972. I was proud to work in the Bureau under J. Edgar Hoover.

My first assignment was Springfield, and I was immediately sent to a Resident Agency in southern Illinois. I was the first black agent assigned to this Division and worked Extremists Matters. This involved Students for a Democratic Society (SDS), Black Panthers, and the Klu Klux Klan. Many of these groups were involved in bombings on college campuses and in high profile crimes aimed at social justice causes. Many of these crimes were committed simply to improve the coffers of those involved under the guise of social justice. Being black worked at a great advantage in many cases, as I could blend in with and work undercover with many of these groups.

I was transferred back to New York City in 1974 which I wanted very badly; always being a New Yorker at heart. I was assigned to reactive squads working Calvin Klein's daughter's kidnapping and major airline industry frauds. I actually developed a Bureau expertise in the latter due to my assignment at the Kennedy Airport Resident Agency. I even contributed to FBI testimony before a Congressional Committe about this subject.

Being in New York means you always get involved in unusual duties. For example, I was attached to protection details of foreign officials and air hijacking cases. I strongly believe in the team concept. I completed my career in service to my colleagues as one of only four Regional Managers/Supervisors of Employee Assistance. I traveled and met with fellow agents in the real work of service in sensitive personnel issues. It was very gratifying.

I retired from the FBI in 2001 with over 30 years of service. Due to the contacts and extraordinary relationships I developed while with the FBI, I have successfully started my own consulting group and work both domestic and abroad. I treasure the ongoing relationships I

have with so many fellow agents. The success of a
life is often measured by your friends. I feel
very successful.

PART TWO

What Applicants Should Know About the FBI

CHAPTER

The History of the FBI

The FBI is one of several law enforcement agencies under the direction of the United States Attorney General and the Department of Justice. Historically, the FBI has quite uniquely maintained its autonomy, and therefore has developed an extraordinary history. The FBI currently has a backlog of over 80,000 applications for the Special Agent's position alone. Given both the praise and criticism it has garnered over the past few years, it still has the respect and attention of the world. To gain a real understanding of the FBI as it is today, you need to have a little background on how it got here.

HOW IT ALL STARTED

Here's something that might surprise you: The man who founded the FBI (often called the Bureau) apparently had a sense of humor.

In 1892, Charles Bonaparte was a speaker at a meeting of the Baltimore Civil Service Reform Association. The speaker who preceded him was Theodore Roosevelt, then the U.S. Civil Service Commissioner. Roosevelt boasted about his reforms in federal law enforcement, and his moves to replace the patronage system with merit standards in hiring. He went on at some length about one innovation: Border Patrol applicants now were required to take marksmanship tests. The best shooters got the jobs.

When Bonaparte at last took the stage, he suggested an even more effective way to weed out Border Patrol candidates: "Roosevelt should have had the men shoot at each other, and given the jobs to the survivors."

All right, so it's not something you'd hear on late night TV, but it's not bad for a lawman. Apparently Roosevelt was impressed; in 1905, just after his reelection to the presidency, he appointed Bonaparte to the Attorney General post.

At that time, the United States was undergoing huge changes economically, socially, and politically. The Industrial Revolution pulled more and more people away from farms and small towns to the big cities. Railroads, and then automobiles, increased mobility across the country. Americans started looking to the federal government—not the states, the towns, or the counties—for help in dealing with problems such as crime.

This was the background of the Progressive political movement. The Progressives argued that only a strong federal system, run by competent professionals, could provide justice in the new industrial society. Roosevelt was a Progressive; so was his new Attorney General.

In 1905, when Bonaparte took office, the Department of Justice had no real investigative force: a few Special Agents reported to the Attorney General and a group of Examiners (trained as accountants) kept an eye on the federal courts' books. If the Department of Justice needed investigators, it hired them from private agencies, or from other government agencies—most often the Secret Service.

Then, in 1908, Congress enacted a law barring the Department of Justice from hiring Secret Service operatives. This was fine with Bonaparte, who preferred to have his investigators reporting to him instead of the Treasury Department, as the Secret Service operatives did. In June 1908, Bonaparte appointed a group of 34 Special Agents within the Department of Justice; on July 26, 1908, he ordered them to report to Chief Examiner Stanley W. Finch. This is marked as the official beginning of the FBI.

On March 16, 1909, Bonaparte's successor, Attorney General George Wickersham, named the force the Bureau of Investigation and changed its leader's title to Chief of the Bureau of Investigation.

The Bureau of Investigation's duties were still fairly vague. At that point, there were few federal crimes. The first Special Agents spent a lot of their time investigating cases of peonage, or involuntary servitude; usually, this happened when someone was forced to "work off" a debt. The Bureau of Investigation also investigated bank fraud cases, antitrust issues, and illegal interstate shipment of liquor. The first major expansion of the Bureau's duties came in 1910, when the Mann Act was passed. This law, also known as the White Slavery Act, made it illegal to transport women across state lines "for immoral purposes."

In 1912, Bureau Chief Finch stepped aside to become Commissioner of White Slavery Act violations, and former Special Examiner A. Bruce Bielaski took his place. Then, as the world lurched toward the Great War, the Bureau's duties really expanded. The Bureau helped the Department of Labor investigate enemy aliens; on its own, the Bureau investigated acts of sabotage and espionage—many of them real, but many others reported by Americans who were becoming almost hysterically suspicious of anything or anyone foreign.

After the war, Americans' xenophobia faded, actual and suspected sabotage disappeared, and the Bureau's duties returned to their prewar scope. In July 1919, William J. Flynn, former head of the Secret Service, became the new Director of the Bureau of Investigation. That October, Congress passed the National Motor Vehicle Theft Act, which soon became the Bureau's major tool in pursuing criminals across state lines.

In 1921, President Warren G. Harding took office, promising to return the country to "normalcy." However, his administration soon became notorious for corruption and graft. Harding's Attorney General replaced Bureau Director Flynn with William J. Burns, an old pal who had operated his own detective agency. The Burns Agency had developed quite a reputation as a strike-breaking organization during the labor wars in the West. Under Burns, the Bureau's ethical standards for hiring and investigations slipped.

Harding died in 1923, in the midst of the Teapot Dome scandal—a case of graft and profiteering that seemed to involve just about everyone in the administration but the president himself. New president Calvin Coolidge was determined to clean house; as part of that cleanup, he demanded the Attorney General's resignation. The new Attorney General, Harlan Fiske Stone, then asked for Burns's resignation as director of the Bureau of Investigation. On May 10, 1924, Stone appointed a new Director—a 29-year-old Department of Justice employee named J. Edgar Hoover.

THE J. EDGAR HOOVER ERA

Hoover is definitely one of the most controversial figures in American history. I know quite a few former agents from the Hoover days who think he was great. Other current and former agents and quite a few people outside the Bureau believe he was overzealous at best and diabolical at worst. This book does not intend to condemn Hoover or to exonerate him, but I want to make my own point of view clear.

I think Hoover did a lot of good for the Bureau, especially in the early days, when it badly needed structure and leadership. However, he did rule with an iron hand. Hoover wanted his Agents to transcend the legacy of corruption found in its early organizational transformations. Many employees were intimidated by his need to control image and performance. Many in his upper circles were afraid to question him or to deviate from his rules and regulations—white shirts, fedoras, and suits to name a familiar one. Hoover's ideas were designed to promote an image of professional and incorruptible agents. However, Hoover stayed too long, and many of those rules proved to be out of sync with society and no longer reflective of modern law enforcement.

For instance, when I first joined the Bureau, there was a rule that agents weren't supposed to be at their desks—ever. They were supposed to be out on the street, working cases. This practice was known as TIO, or Time in Office. You were supposed to keep TIO down. Hoover thought controlling TIO would bolster the image that agents were on the job 24 hours a day, 7 days a week. When I got to my second posting, in Milwaukee, I sat down at my desk to get organized. The Special Agent in Charge said, "Douglas, what are you doing? Get out of here!"

I just looked at him and said, "Where am I supposed to go? I don't have a car, I don't have any cases yet."

"I don't care, just get out of here. You're not supposed to be here!"

So I went outside and started wandering around, just window shopping. You could spot all the FBI agents in their suits and white shirts walking the streets of downtown Milwaukee. Agents would have to duck into public phone booths to make calls, and would do much of our paperwork in the public library. We didn't get as much accomplished as we should, given these odd rules.

Blind obedience like that is a dangerous environment for any organization. But Hoover's vision squelched the historical notion that law enforcement officals were controlled by the politicians. His rules and regulations were meant to show citizens that the FBI stood for professionalism, incorruptibility, and excellence. After his death in 1972, many changes occurred as were necessary. I know from personal experience the Bureau does a damn good job of making improvements when needed. Does the Bureau make mistakes? Absolutely—it is an organization of individuals and agendas just like any large corporation. The Bureau often takes a big hit in the media because it sets standards and principles high for law enforcement, but then is not able to openly discuss its failings more honestly with the public. Excesses and missteps have occurred, but the Bureau has always taken steps to safeguard against them for the future.

Okay, that's the end of the sermon; back to the history lesson.

Hoover took over the Bureau of Investigation just as the Gangster Era began. This was the time of Bonnie and Clyde, of Eliot Ness and the Untouchables (who, incidentally, were Treasury Agents). Prohibition opened up new possibilities for crime, and made criminals of many otherwise ordinary Americans. However, even in the middle of a bull market in criminal activity, the Bureau didn't have as much to do as you might think; its jurisdiction was much, much smaller than it is today. The Bureau did investigate Al Capone as a "fugitive federal witness," and it used the Mann Act to bring a philandering Ku Klux Klan "Imperial Kleagle" to justice.

One of J. Edgar Hoover's first projects was a major overhaul in the way the Bureau was run. When he took over, the Bureau of Investigation had approximately 650 employees, including 441 Special Agents. He immediately fired agents he considered unqualified, abolished the seniority rule of promotion, and set up standard performance appraisals. He scheduled regular inspections of Headquarters and field office operations. He developed more stringent standards for hiring, and in January 1928 he established a formal training course for new agents. By the end of the decade, the Identification Division was up and running. The Bureau of Investigation was renamed the United States Bureau of Investigation on July 1, 1932.

That same year, the Bureau established its Technical Laboratory. In a story about the new lab, journalist Rex Collier called it "a novel research laboratory where government criminologists will match wits with underworld cunning." Originally the small lab operated strictly as a research facility. Eventually, it offered specialized microscopes for examining forensic evidence, plus an extensive reference collections of guns, watermarks, typefaces, and automobile tire designs. This was the beginning of the Bureau's now-legendary laboratory capability.

THE BUREAU'S JURISDICTION EXPANDS

Necessity is the mother of invention. Criminal activites moved across geographic and statutory boundaries, forcing the Bureau to change its jurisdiction. The Bureau was relegated to the sidelines of one of the century's most spectacular crimes: the 1932 kidnapping and murder of the Lindbergh baby. No federal criminal statutes existed that covered kidnapping, so the Bureau had no jurisdiction; the case was handled by local police. Later that year, Congress passed a kidnapping statute that set the death penalty for transporting a victim across state lines. However the law had no presumptive clause, which would automatically make kidnapping a federal crime. In 1934, the law was amended, calling for federal intervention if the kidnapping case was not solved within seven days. In the 1950s, that period of time was shortened to 24 hours, after another kidnapping death of an infant. Finally, after more and more of these cases, lawmakers realized immediate intervention was vital. Today, the FBI is authorized to step in immediately to investigate a kidnapping or any crime involving a child.

But the Bureau of Investigation did make a name for itself with high-profile shoot-outs involving criminals such as John Dillinger, Baby Face Nelson, and Pretty Boy Floyd. In 1934, President Roosevelt used these and other spectacular crimes to push through several laws expanding the Bureau's jurisdiction. New federal crimes included the killing or assault of a federal officer, extortion involving interstate commerce, kidnapping with no ransom demand, crossing state lines to escape prosecution or avoid giving testimony, robbery of any bank operating under federal rules, and interference with interstate commerce through violence, intimidation or threats. Finally, the Bureau's **agents** were given full police powers to arrest and apprehend suspects, plus the right to carry firearms at all times while on duty.

In 1935, Bureau was officially named the Federal Bureau of Investigation. At this time, Hoover has the forsight to understand that interagency relations would be pivotal, and oversaw the creation of the FBI National

Academy to begin training local and state police officers. The political capital this afforded Hoover did not escape him, nor did the opportunity to place the FBI as the premier law enforcement agency in the country.

By 1936, the country was focused on in impending economic depression, and the world overseas was becoming incresingly unstable. The American Communist Party found ready membership, given the environment of labor unrest, racial disturbances, and sympathy for Spanish Loyalists fighting Franco's Facists. President Roosevelt authorized the FBI to investigate these organizations as threats to national security.

War broke out in Europe in 1939. A Presidential directive strengthened the FBI's authority to investigate subversive activity in the United States; subversion, sabotage, and espionage became major targets of FBI investigations. At least one FBI Agent trained in defense plant protection was placed in each of the FBI's 42 field offices. The FBI developed intelligence networks of informants through fraternal and veterans' organizations. Leads developed through these networks, and through their own work, helped Special Agents investigate potential threats to national security and initiated its mission regarding national security issues.

THE FBI AND WORLD WAR II

France fell to the Germans in 1940, and Great Britain became virtually the only opponent to the Axis forces. Under the direction of Russia, the American Communist Party pushed for U.S. neutrality. But through 1940 and 1941, the country increased aid to Great Britain and the Allies. In late 1940, Congress reestablished the draft, and the FBI started tracking down draft evaders and deserters.

The FBI participated in destroying one of the biggest wartime spy rings discovered—the operation led to the arrest and conviction of 33 people. The key to the case was a man named William Sebold. He was born in Germany, left the country in 1921, settled in the United States, and became a citizen in 1936. When he returned to Germany for a visit in 1939; the Gestapo seized him and threatened his family, trying to force him to become a spy.

Sebold agreed, but then contacted the American consulate in Cologne and offered to become a double agent. Sebold returned home to Long Island, and the FBI set up his spy shop. Sebold was given a short-wave radio and a business office fitted with surveillance devices. FBI agents also studied the microfilm Sebold was given in Germany and discovered codes and instructions that led to spies already operating in the United States.

For months, Sebold took instructions from Germany, passed them along to the FBI, and then sent back misleading information carefully designed to seem authentic. In June 1941, the FBI pulled in the net and arrested 33 suspects.

Later that month, on June 22, Hitler's troops attacked Russia—without warning, and in violation of the Nazi-Soviet pact. American Communists became less of a threat, and the FBI focused more and more on potentially dangerous German, Italian, and Japanese nationals, and native-born Americans who worked to assist the Axis. Then, on December 7, 1941, the Japanese bombed the American naval base at Pearl Harbor, Hawaii. President Roosevelt declared the country's entry into World War II the next day.

One of the most shameful episodes of World War II was the internment of Japanese nationals and American citizens of Japanese descent. The FBI had already arrested specific individuals who posed security threats, and Hoover argued that the large-scale internment wasn't necessary. However, President Roosevelt and the Attorney General supported the military's recommendation. Ultimately, the FBI became responsible for arresting curfew and evacuation violators.

In April 1945, President Roosevelt died and Vice President Harry Truman took office as President. Before the end of the month, Hitler committed suicide. In May 1945, Germany's surrender brought peace in Europe, but war raged on through the Pacific. Truman made the decision to use atomic weapons in Japan, and the last Axis power surrendered on August 14, 1945.

THE FIFTIES

The 1950s brought peace and prosperity, but also anxiety. It was a time of police professionalization and an increasing reliance on the FBI. The United States was the world's richest, most powerful nation. But the memories of war and the new horror unleashed at Hiroshima made Americans fearful. When the Soviets detonated their own atomic bomb in 1949, counteracting the Communist threat became a paramount focus of government at all levels.

While U.S. foreign policy concentrated on defeating Communist expansion abroad, many Americans worried about the Communist threat at home. In 1939 and again in 1943, Presidential directives had authorized the FBI to carry out investigations of threats to national security. This role was clarified and expanded under Presidents Truman and Eisenhower. Anyone with information about subversive activities was urged to report it to the FBI. The Bureau distributed a poster on the program to police departments across the country. One of the poster's points, often ignored, warned Americans to "avoid reporting malicious gossip or idle rumors."

During this time, Special Agent Frank Watts worked in Connecticut, identifying Soviet agents spying at a navy yard there. Here's one story he shared:

Frank Watts: The Case of the Spy Next Door

```
        Often we'd start with surveillance of a Soviet
    diplomat, and we'd watch him make contact with
    several other individuals. That's when it became
    very intriguing—trying to determine who that
```

individual was, why he was contacted, what that individual might furnish as far as secret documents.

I was the Senior Resident Agent in Stamford, Connecticut, covering most all of the Soviet illegal espionage activities in the area. One of my neighbors—I'll call him John Doe—had a son who was the same age as my son, both of them about eight years old. The boys went to Scouts together, so this neighbor and I both became active in Boy Scouts. We got to be pretty close friends; his wife and my wife did things together, and we visited back and forth. I always thought he was a little pushy, maybe overly friendly. But a nice guy. He was the editor and publisher of a technical magazine out of New York.

Well, one day I was working surveillance on one of the diplomatic officials of the Soviet Union. He left the embassy in New York and came up to White Plains, to meet with one of his agents. We covered that site very discreetly—we had enough information to set it up ahead of time, and we knew this meeting was supposed to be with someone who was passing information.

So the diplomat stepped off the train and went to the telephone booth with his Life magazine under his arm, and stood there in the phone booth a minute. And then John Doe, my next-door neighbor, walked right up and made contact with him.

I wanted to go interview John immediately and double him if I could. And I thought I could. But Director Hoover and others in Washington felt it wasn't the time. I had to continue my relationship with him, because we didn't want him to know that we knew what he was up to.

After that, John came in my office at least twice a week for several months. He'd come in with his big briefcase, and sit down, and talk about nothing. We'd sit there and just talk, and talk some more, and then he would leave.

Then one day, John's principal—the diplomat we'd followed—was arrested in New Jersey, clearing a drop box. Of course, this made headlines in the papers, and we knew John would see it and that would have a definite effect on him. So I was told to go ahead and make contact.

John boarded the New Haven—New York commuter train every day. So I got on the train ahead of him. I had a paper folded up under my arm, one of the tabloids with this principal's picture in it. When I saw John sit down, I sat down with him, and we chatted for a minute. Then I opened up the paper. You could see John's reaction—he just got extremely nervous right away.

When we got into Grand Central, John said, "Well, Frank, I'll see you later."

And I said, "I'm afraid not. You've got to go with me." He just sighed real big and said, "I knew that was coming."

We went down to the New York office, and had two or three days of productive interviews. John cooperated completely. He told me the reason he kept coming by my office was because he was trying to get himself to confess and become a double agent for us.

John had been convinced to hand over something pretty minor. And when he did that, they pushed it a step further, then a step further, and then started paying him for information. Because he was the publisher and editor of this technical magazine, he had access to places off limits to most people. One of those places was the jet propulsion laboratory in California. He went there and obtained some information the Soviets wanted, and passed it along for a price. Then he became a fully active agent.

John turned out to be a good double agent. He got a new principal; it took a year or so before they made their contact with him, but they did. John was able to furnish us some valuable information about that principals and about people who were passing on identity documents to support KGB agents that might be coming in: driver's

```
licenses, marriage licenses, birth certificates,
and so forth.
     Things were never quite the same in Boy Scout
meetings, though.
```

The 1950s also proved to be a time of domestic problems. One developing crime problem was the Mafia. In 1957, the New York State Police discovered many of the country's best-known mobsters had met in upstate New York for what is well known as the Appalachian Meeting. The FBI, with the New York State Police, collected information on all the individuals identified at the meeting and confirmed the existence of a national organized crime network. But legal remedies were slow in coming, until an FBI agent convinced mob insider Joseph Valachi to testify before a Senate subcommittee on organized crime. Valachi's testimony in September 1963 galvanized public opinion. In response, Congress passed two new laws to strengthen existing federal racketeering and gambling statutes.

The FBI also continued to pursue organized crime activities as they transformed into many faces: Russian mafia, American street gangs, and Colombian and Chinese gangs to name a few.

History of the "Top Ten"

I don't want to claim undue credit for the FBI, but I'm pretty sure the Bureau was one of the first to popularize the "Top Ten" countdown with its Ten Most Wanted Fugitives Program.

The first FBI list was compiled in March 1950, in response to a reporter's question. A writer for International News Service, the predecessor to United Press International, asked the FBI for the names and descriptions of the "toughest guys" they had targeted. The story was a big hit. J. Edgar Hoover always had a gift for publicizing the Bureau, so he decided to make the list a regular program. On March 14, 1950, the Ten Most Wanted Fugitives Program was implemented. Since then, almost 7,000 of the listed fugitives have been captured.

Over the years, as the types of crimes the FBI focuses on have changed, the types of fugitives the FBI pursued have changed, too. During the 1950s, most of the criminals on the list were bank robbers, burglars, and car thieves. During the radical 1960s, the list included leftist revolutionaries, such as the Weathermen. In a criminal reflection of the growing women's movement, Ruth Eisemann-Schier became first woman on the list; she debuted in 1968 for charges including kidnapping and extortion. In the 1970s, the Ten Most Wanted were mainly involved in organized crime and terrorism. Today, serial murderers and drug kingpins have joined the bombers and mobsters. The current Top Ten list is populated by murderers, drug dealers, terrorists, one burgler, and a child molester. The Top Ten tends to reflect society at large.

In May 1998, the first million-dollar reward was offered for information leading to the capture of a Ten-Most-Wanted fugitive; Eric Robert Rudolph is a suspect in the January 29, 1998, bombing of an abortion clinic in Birmingham, Alabama. A Birmingham police officer who had been moonlighting as a security guard was killed in the explosion, and a nurse who worked at the clinic was seriously wounded and nearly blinded.

How does the FBI choose the ten fugitives for the list? There are two criteria. First, the fugitive is considered particularly dangerous, which may be reflected either in a long record of serious crimes or involvement in a few extremely heinous incidents. Second, the Bureau believes nationwide publicity will help catch the fugitive. Special Agents of the Criminal Investigative Division (CID) who keep up with all current FBI fugitives make preliminary recommendations, working with representatives from the Bureau's Office of Public and Congressional Affairs (OPCA) who coordinate fugitive publicity. The FBI's field offices across the country also submit recommendations. The selection is approved by the Assistant Director of CID, the Inspector in Charge of OPCA, and finally, by the Director.

Unless a Top Ten Fugitive is captured, found dead, or surrenders, he or she is removed from the list for only two reasons. Either the criminal charges are dropped, or the fugitive no longer fits the "Top Ten" criteria listed above. The FBI posts the Ten Most Wanted list on its website at www.fbi.gov.

Following the events of September 11, the FBI also generated a "Terrorists Most Wanted List." There is no magic number to limit this list. All individuals listed have been indicted by Federal Grand Juries, and will remain on the list until they are brought to justice or they are definitively understood to be deceased.

THE SIXTIES AND SEVENTIES

Racism, one of the deep-rooted injustices of American society, really came to the forefront during the '50s and '60s. After fighting for their country in World War II and Korea, black Americans wouldn't stand for the Jim Crow segregation of the past.

The Civil Rights Movement

During most of this time, the FBI had no jurisdiction over civil rights violations, no matter how brutal or blatant. The turning point came in the summer of 1964, when Michael Schwerner, Andrew Goodman, and James Cheney were murdered near Philadelphia, Mississippi. The three young voter-registration workers disappeared shortly after they were released from the city jail. Their bodies were found weeks later, buried in a levee.

The Department of Justice ordered an FBI investigation. The case worked its way through the courts for years. In 1966, the Supreme Court broadened its interpretation of civil rights law and made it clear that federal agencies could investigate and prosecute civil rights violations. Seven men were eventually found guilty of the murders of Schwerner, Goodman, and Cheney. In the meantime, the FBI began taking steps to deal with the turmoil in the South, sending in agents to deal specifically with civil rights unrest.

Frank Watts was one of those agents, and he tells an amazing story about one of his encounters with an especially violent racist, Tommy Tarrants. (Frank's story, along with other from the era is told in more detail in the book *Terror in the Night: The Klan's Campaign Against the Jews,* by Jack Nelson.)

Frank Watts: Catching the Man from the Klan

I'd been in Connecticut for over ten years at that point, working mostly espionage, when I was sent back to Mississippi. One particular Klan group, the White Knights of the Ku Klux Klan, was really spreading havoc throughout the South, and particularly in Mississippi.

At that time, the FBI did not have an office in Mississippi. The northern part of the state was covered out of Memphis, the southern part out of New Orleans. In 1964, President Johnson instructed Hoover to open up an office in Mississippi, specifically because of this Klan activity. They'd bombed and burned churches and synagogues, disrupted the voter registration activity. Several people had been killed, including three civil rights workers. This was the FBI's major crisis at that time.

So Hoover came down, opened the office, and sent in 100 FBI agents to handle the problem, in Mississippi and several of the southern states. Anything else took a back seat. Of course there wasn't that much else going on in Mississippi, at that point.

Quite a few of us who were sent down were from the South. It was easier to get people to cooperate if you were a Southerner. I think the local people felt that we weren't outsiders, we understood their situation. That made it a little easier to sit down and talk to them and let them see how this violence and bigotry was just not the answer. And that was the most important thing, getting people to cooperate and talk to us. That was how we were really able to penetrate the Klan.

Of course the Klan had real severe penalties for anyone who cooperated with the FBI. It was difficult for some of these people to do it, to speak to us. They were really putting their lives in danger.

Things shifted when the Bureau solved the murders of those three civil rights workers: Cheney, Goodman, and Schwerner. The Klan leaders were indicted, as well as the ones that actually pulled the triggers. Now, none of them could do anything openly. They knew they were under surveillance, and if they did anything out of the ordinary, any further Klan activity, their bond would be revoked, and they'd go off to jail. They had to get outsiders to do the dirty work.

That's when Tommy Tarrants, this young boy from Mobile, Alabama, came into the picture. He'd attended a few Klan meetings in Alabama, but he'd never been in any trouble with the law. He saw the need of carrying on the Klan activity, so he got in his car and came over to Mississippi to visit with Sam Bowers, the head of the White Knights. Sam was under indictment, and Tommy volunteered his services. Of course, Bowers didn't feel this boy was legitimate, and thought maybe he was an FBI informant. So Sam just thanked him and sent him on his way.

Tommy then went out and did some bombings on his own—burned up some black churches and bombed a rabbi's home. Just to show Bowers that he was really who he said he was, you know. The only injury at this point occurred when he shot into the home of a black civil rights leader, just outside of Jackson, and injured a little girl in the leg. Fortunately, she wasn't badly hurt, but these were significant bombings. Lot of damage, very frightening.

Sam took Tommy seriously at that point, and the Klan set up what they called an underground hit squad. It was composed of six individuals, including Tommy Tarrants, who was the leader of this group. They wouldn't go to meetings or anything; their only contact with the Klan would be through very trusted members. That's how they'd get instructions, monies, and so forth.

This squad started out with bank robberies, in order to get money. They bought ammunition and supplies, and two automobiles. They then began to do the work of casing places to get the information they needed, prior to any bombings or burnings.

At this point, we knew a group existed, but not much else. I was sent to gather intelligence, and that's what we worked on through 1966 and 1967. It was a tough thing to do, but we'd get little tidbits of this, little tidbits of that. That the group was about to do this or that. But we didn't know who was in the group or how it was organized. And we had no idea who the leader was. We had lots and lots of information about the leader's automobile, about his being spotted near violent activity. We were building a file, but the identities of the people involved were just completely unknown to us.

The information we were receiving got more extreme as time went on. The bombings were getting to be more heinous, more focused on actually hurting people instead of just causing property damage. The Klan group started out burning black churches that had someone actively registering voters. It was fairly easy for them to go there in the dark of night and burn those churches.

Then they switched targets and concentrated on Jews. The Klan felt there was a Jewish, Communist conspiracy behind the blacks to support the civil rights work. The squad bombed the Temple Beth Israel synagogue in Jackson, Mississippi, and another synagogue over in

Meridien, Mississippi. They burned two rabbis'
homes. They were still burning black churches
out in the rural areas, but that activity was
really reduced.

We were still investigating all these
activities, and activities all over Mississippi.
We had another killing down in Hattiesburg,
Mississippi. Vernon Dahmer was an outstanding
individual, a fine man, actively engaged in
voter registration. They came in and burned his
house and killed him. So we were actively
investigating that, and at the same time we were
trying to get information to stay a step ahead of
this underground hit squad.

That was the real problem, and it was my
problem: Trying to stay a step ahead, in order to
abort anything that they'd planned. We were
walking along with information from members of
the Klan, but they weren't the high-up, trusted
ones. We weren't getting the information we
really needed, from the inside sources.

And then a Jewish businessman by the name of
Meyer Davidson became involved. He had a very
outstanding family there in Meridien. They'd
done so much for the city, built a baseball
complex, and this, that and the other—just a
very fine, civic-minded family. It was his
synagogue that the Klan had blown up. Meyer
Davidson offered a $70,000 payment to anyone who

had information that led to a solution and a successful prosecution.

Well, that incensed them, this Klan group. They'd decided they'd bomb his house, murder him and his family. And then they received orders to bomb the Temple Beth Israel synagogue again, this time during the services. You can imagine how many people would be killed then. Women and children and all.

That's what we heard through our sources—this plan was on the drawing board. That was just a little bit too much for us to take, you know. We didn't know when, or how, or by whom. Just that this underground squad was planning these very violent bombings, designed to kill.

We still didn't know who the leader of the group was, this man we later found out was Tommy Tarrants. The informants didn't know his name, either. They just referred to him as The Man. And so we referred to him as The Man, because we had no other identification. We had a pretty good physical description, but that's all.

We knew we had to have much better information coming from more trusted Klan people, closer to the leaders. We started going to our sources to find out from them who would know what we needed to know. And we just had to have that information ahead of time. We could not allow this activity to take place.

94

We went through all our sources, good ones, bad ones, mediocre ones. We talked to all of them to try to find our targets, and we found two individuals, brothers. They were both in the Klan, and one was reportedly involved in the civil rights murders—Goodman, Cheney and Schwerner. These two brothers were very much in on the Klan's planning and they knew about all the activities.

So we made contact with these brothers and let them know that we had to have this information. I demanded that they come to my house, so we could sit down and have an understanding. Well, they did show up, with their attorney. Even with the attorney there, they laid it on the line—that they did have this information, but their lives were in danger if they divulged it.

We met night after night in a little mobile home out in the woods. Had a real prayer meeting about two or three times a week—the brothers, their attorney, me, a couple of other agents, some of the local detectives. Those brothers would lay their guns out on the table, we'd lay ours out, and then we'd pray.

It was touch-and-go for several weeks. They never would give us the name of The Man; they always claimed didn't know for sure. But they let us know that the Klan decided that before they did the job on the synagogue, making the big splash of killing all these people, they'd take care of Meyer Davidson first. That was really a thorn in their side, this man putting up all this money to stop them.

These brothers knew they might be in a position to get that money, so that was a help. But what really brought them around was, they were convinced that we could take action, and we would take action—action against them, if they didn't cooperate. We had to fight fire with fire. It was completely different from what I had done in New York, with the espionage cases. That was a lot of finesse, trying to match wits with these people who had seven years of training. Any success there came about through careful planning and finesse.

But with the Klan, you were dealing with people who—well, Hoover called them rednecks. And they were. Uneducated, and extremely violent. We saw early on there was no place for finesse. And so they knew that we were dead serious, we were going to take action against them if anything happened. We just got them in a corner where they realized the only way out would be to cooperate and prevent these bombings.

So finally they did give us some information, first of all about the targets the

Klan had in mind. The Klan had this little code
for what they'd do to people—Number One was your
basic harassment, like a nasty telephone call.
Number Two was throwing a dead chicken on the
porch, something of that nature. Number Three
was a beating. And Number Four was a killing.
Several of us in the FBI were on the list for a
Number Four. So was Meyer Davidson, of course,
and another Jewish businessman there in town,
and the chief of police of Meridien. Of course we
were relying on these brothers to let us know who
was going to be first.

They did come through on this particular
Saturday afternoon, June 30, 1968. They called
me and said, "This is it. They're in town, and
The Man's here too. He's got a woman with him
that's done all the case work, all the
preparation for the bombings. They're headed for
Meyer Davidson's." Then the brothers said they
were going to set up their alibi, which was to go
to a nightclub and start a fight so they'd get
arrested and be in jail when the bombing
happened.

Of course, we were covering all the targeted
areas already. I immediately got the Davidson
family out of the house, and we set up good
roadblocks all over. The people who lived across
the street let us take over their house, just

moved out for the weekend. And so we were able to set up a good cover.

We knew dynamite was involved, because it had been involved in all the other bombings. We'd called in some dynamite experts from Fort Benning, Georgia, and had them available. So that night we were all set up when they came in.

Tommy Tarrants, he was The Man. Kathy Ainsworth was the woman with him, a married school teacher who'd moved up from Miami. Her husband knew she was in the Klan, but he couldn't get her to leave. She said she'd leave him if he tried to make her leave the Klan. So she kept her activities up, and she did a lot of the preparation work, examining the sites the Klan had picked out.

Shortly after 11:30 that night, they drove up in a nice Buick automobile. This was a little unusual because the Klan used to travel in pickup trucks with shotguns in the back. Turns out this was one of the cars they bought with money from the early bank robberies. Kathy Ainsworth was driving.

Tommy got out of the car, carrying a box. We could tell it was heavy, by the way he was bent down with it. He had 29 sticks of dynamite in there—unstable, highly explosive. In fact, the box was leaking; the dynamite was almost pure nitroglycerine. The bomb experts from Fort

Benning said that if that stuff had gone off, it would've blown up seven houses all around, including the house we were in across the street.

So Tommy carried that box over and got under the bedroom window. And he began to place his dynamite on the timing device. It was all set up, except for the wires. All Tommy had to do was attach the wires. He couldn't do that while he was traveling, you know. As he started do that we moved in. We hollered, "FBI! Don't move!" and he turned. He had a .45, and he started firing.

Tommy was an excellent marksman. A lot of the Klan were. They'd go out and practice in a big gravel pit over in Jackson, day after day, for months. But the one thing that they neglected to do was practice at night. Your only light source at night is the sky, so you tend to shoot high.

Well, at Quantico, we had all kinds of firearms training, including how to shoot at night, without a light. We knew how to compensate for that. So Tommy was shooting over our heads, and we were shooting right at him.

We're trained not to shoot to kill, but shoot to capture. The first shot, I got him the leg, just above his knee, and dynamite went all over the place. Tommy hurried back to the car, got to the nearest door. We hit him as he reached the car door, and took a big chunk out of his arm.

Kathy was shot in the neck and killed instantly.
Tommy got in the car, pushed her over, got behind
the wheel and took off.

He just went around the first roadblock, and
they were shooting at the back of the Buick. In
1968, most cars had balloon cushion tires, with
an inner tube. You could run over a nail, and it
wouldn't go down. We kept shooting at his tires,
trying to get him to stop. He went 15 blocks
before those tires went down. Finally, he
couldn't negotiate a turn and ran up in
someone's yard. The police captain was in the
car right behind, when Tommy got out of his car
and turned his machine gun on him. Tommy hit the
captain three times, including once in the
heart. And the captain lived.

One of the neighbors there came out on his
porch, to see what was going on. Tommy shot him in
the stomach, and then went on back behind the house.
That man lived, too.

A policeman came up right behind the first
car and made his way behind the house, to the
field back there. This family was raising German
shepherds, and they had the fence electrified.
Tommy kept trying to go over the fence, and it
kept knocking him down. By the time we got to
him, he was laying there, just bleeding. He
looked like just a bloody rag, really.

At that point we put him in the ambulance, along with Kathy Ainsworth, although she was already deceased. I sent one agent to the hospital with him, in order to take a dying declaration. I was sure he couldn't live. In case he talked before he died, I wanted someone there to take it down, because dying declarations are admissible in court.

But Tommy never would talk. He got to the hospital, and he lived.There was a real excellent doctor in Meridien who'd made a lot of progress in orthopedic surgery, using pins, that kind of thing. He operated on Tommy's arm and all, and he was able to save the arm. Patched him up pretty well.

Of course Tommy was tried on the state charge, for bombing an occupied dwelling. The FBI cooperated as much as we could, but it was up to the state to handle the prosecution. He was found guilty and sent to the state penitentiary.

Throughout all this, during the investigation and the trial, Tommy Tarrants was totally unrepentant. I interviewed him 36 times and never got anything from him. I really wanted to get him to testify, because if he did, then I felt we could put at least another 28 people in prison. But he never would.

About 16 months after Tommy went to prison, he escaped with the help of the Klan—he and a partner, who wasn't a Klansman. Tommy and his buddy got themselves into the prison hospital, then they knocked a hospital worker over the head with a lead pipe. Then the Klan picked them up behind the prison grounds and they took off down to Jackson, Mississippi. The Klan had set up a little lean-to tent there at the edge of the airport, with food and money and a change of clothes for them. They were ready to hijack an airplane and go to Nova Scotia.

But we were able to surround the tent and move in while they were still inside. They opened fire on us, and we returned fire. Tommy's buddy was killed, but Tommy's life was spared.

Well, Tommy went back to prison, and got two years in solitary confinement for the escape. He was put in a six-by-eight cell, where he could come out twice a week for a shower, and that was it. I continued my interviews with him, kept going to see him there in prison.

I really saw a troubled youth, you know? And he was just about the same age as my older son. I could see how messed up Tommy was. All he wanted was his Bible, so I took that to him. He was using the Bible to justify his Klan activities— completely off-base. We'd argue back and forth. But I was really the only one who could come and talk to him. His family would come, but they weren't allowed to visit with him.

I was just trying to get him to testify. Tommy was really hard at that time. But I believe he came to enjoy me visiting with him. We'd talk about everything—his life in general, and religion. My wife and her church group began a prayer vigil for him. She'd give me little tracts and things to give to Tommy.

And you know, he was appreciative. It was something to do, and something to read. He began reading philosophy and things like that, too. Of course he had plenty of time. Nothing but time.

After a while, he really had a born-again experience. He wrote a letter to the *New York Times*, telling people engaged in violent activity that that wasn't the answer. The *Times* published that letter, although they did make a mistake. Tommy had just put "MSU" on the address, which stood for Maximum Security Unit. The article they ran along with the letter said that Tommy had written from Mississippi State University. I got a chuckle out of that.

One of the things we did in the FBI was keep up with the daily papers. You'd clip anything that had thing to do with an FBI case and send it down to Washington, where it would be put in the case file.

When that story hit Hoover's desk, he called me and requested, or demanded, that I get up to the penitentiary and talk with Tommy. Hoover thought this conversion was another ploy to help him escape.

So of course I went right on up. This time, when Tommy came out, I could see that he was completely different. He said, "Frank, I appreciate what you've done for me and all. I want you to know, I'm not the same person I was."

Of course I was leery at first. But I realized it wasn't the jailhouse religion that a lot of people get, because he wasn't wanting anything. That was one of the first things I asked him. What do you want out of this? Are you doing this to get out? And he said, "No, I've accepted Christ. I don't want anything else." I went to the chaplain there, and he then observed Tommy closely, and talked with him. And he felt like I did, that this was a true conversion.

I went to some of the leaders in the Jewish community and the black community and asked them to go visit him, just to find out if they saw what I did. I felt that if he really had changed, he could do more good outside than in. And I was going to do what I could do to get him out.

One of the first people I visited was a prominent Jewish lawyer in Jackson, Mississippi, by the name of Al Binder. He used to bring me the money over to Meridien to pay the informers. He was a target of the Klan, because of his prominence. After a lot of persuasion on my part, he agreed to go see Tommy.

Al Binder sits down and Tommy says, "Let me draw you a picture of your house." He had it right down to pinpoint accuracy: How to get in Al Binder's house, where to place the bomb, and so forth. Al told me later, "It really got my attention." But then Tommy asked him for forgiveness.

Al became convinced Tommy was sincere, and he had a lot more pull than I did in the state of Mississippi. In fact, he was the legal advisor for the governor at the time. He was able to help in getting Tommy paroled. Senator John Stennis, who's deceased now, had a secretary who was a lawyer there in Jackson. The secretary went to interview Tommy and he was able to help. He was convinced. Everybody was convinced except my boss, Hoover. He told me, "If anything happens, I'll hold you personally responsible."

I knew that I was risking my job and everything else, but I was convinced that Tommy really had changed, and he could do some real good on the outside. In the meantime, he was teaching other inmates and reaching out to people who had been in his situation, trying to get them to see that violence was not the answer.

During this whole time, he never gave me the names of the other men who'd been in the underground hit squad with him. Never did. The way he explained it to me, he'd talked so many of these people into doing these things, convinced them to go along, that he felt it wouldn't be right to give me their names. He didn't want to get out of prison by putting other people in.

Well, after this started hitting the papers, we'd start getting phone calls. A Klansman would call up and say, "I know what happened. I read the papers. I know what Tommy was doing, trying to bomb the synagogue and bomb these homes and so forth. I don't want any more part of the Klan. You'll find my robe under an oak tree out on Highway 23."

Tommy wrote a letter to the paper there in Jackson, Mississippi, stating that he had never talked to us about the bombings, never given names to the FBI. He said had no intention of doing so, unless there was more violence. Tommy said the minute the Klan undertook more acts of violence, he'd go to the FBI and cooperate completely. He told me if lives were in danger, he would cooperate with me and put the people responsible in prison. But as long as the people he had worked with stayed away from violence, he wasn't going to give me information just for personal gain.

Well, Tommy was paroled on December 13, 1976. He took classes at Ole Miss for while, then

```
moved up North and worked with Chuck Colson on
his prison ministry. Then he and some others
there in Washington, DC formed an urban school
for young ministers. He's been active in that
until just this past year. He's taken a year off
to get his doctorate.
      He's still out there, still doing good work.
I'm glad I didn't ever have to go to Mr. Hoover
and say, "Sir, I made a mistake. I was wrong about
Tommy Tarrants."
```

The Vietnam War

While the 1960s counterculture was mostly peaceful, there was a violent edge to some protests. In 1970 alone, there were approximately 3,000 bombings and 50,000 bomb threats in the United States. Two of the most violent incidents of the Vietnam War era took place during that same year.

On May 4, 1970, approximately 300 students and activists gathered at Kent State University to stage a demonstration against the Vietnam War. National Guardsmen were on hand, at the governor's request; after the students refused to disperse and began throwing tear gas canisters back at the troops, the Guardsmen opened fire into the crowd. Thirteen students were wounded; four were killed.

Months later, in the very early morning of August 24, 1970, a powerful explosive destroyed a building on campus at the University of Wisconsin at Madison. Sterling Hall housed the Army Math Research Center, the target of the terrorists. A graduate student was killed and three others were injured.

If Kent State had outraged the left, the bombing in Madison showed the horror and futility of violence in retaliation. Draft dodging and property damage seemed tolerable, even reasonable, to many antiwar sympathizers. Deaths were something different, clearly beyond any reasonable boundary.

Even so, a few violent groups such as the Weathermen continued their operations from an increasingly isolated underground. The FBI dealt with these threats as it had those from Communists and the KKK—using traditional investigative techniques and a series of counterintelligence programs (nicknamed "Cointelpro"). These measures were intended to fight domestic terrorism and gather intelligence on those who threatened terroristic violence. Some of the Cointelpro operations were later found to overstep citizens' right to privacy; this is one reason why wiretapping and other intrusive investigative techniques are now so thoroughly regulated by FBI and Department of Justice guidelines.

Watergate and New Appointments

On May 2, 1972, J. Edgar Hoover died at the age of 77; he was just a few months away from marking his 48th year as FBI Director. President Nixon appointed L. Patrick Gray as Acting Director the day after Hoover's death.

Not long after that, five men were arrested photographing documents at the Democratic National Headquarters in the Watergate Office Building in Washington, DC.

The break-in had been authorized by Republican Party officials working to reelect Nixon. Within hours, the White House was scrambling to cover up its role. Gray's personal connections to Nixon drew him into the Watergate scandal; he withdrew his name from consideration to be Director, and resigned on April 27, 1973.

William Ruckleshaus, a former Congressman and the first head of the Environmental Protection Agency, took over as Acting Director until Clarence Kelley's appointment on July 9, 1973. Kelley was the Kansas City

Police Chief at the time of his appointment, and had been an FBI Agent from 1940 to 1961.

By now, the country was reeling from the Watergate scandal. Americans had become deeply cynical and wary of anything to do with government, including law enforcement. Director Kelley worked to restore public trust in the FBI.

In 1974, he instituted Career Review Boards and programs to identify and train potential managers within the FBI. Through the new National Executive Institute at the FBI National Academy, Kelley also sought to increase professionalism in law enforcement agencies across the country.

Kelley also had to deal with the fallout from public disclosures of the Cointelpro excesses. A Congressional committee investigated the investigators, deciding whether or not the FBI's programs had violated Constitutional rights.

In response to the hearings, Attorney General Edward Levi established specific guidelines in this area—the first time such guidelines had ever been established. Foreign counterintelligence guidelines went into effect on March 10, 1976, and domestic security investigations became effective April 5, 1976. (The domestic guidelines were superseded March 21, 1983.)

Kelley's biggest innovation was "quality over quantity" management. Under Hoover, agents and field offices were expected to handle a certain number of cases each year—a sort of criminal quota. Now, each field office set its own investigative priorities based on the types of crime most prevalent in its territory. The FBI as a whole established three national priorities: foreign counterintelligence, organized crime, and white-collar crime.

In 1978, Director Kelley resigned and was replaced by former federal Judge William H. Webster. In 1982, Webster made counterterrorism a fourth national priority, responding to a rise in international terrorism.

THE EIGHTIES

A new threat surfaced in the '80s—the illegal drug trade. To meet the challenge, in 1982 the Attorney General gave the FBI concurrent jurisdiction with the Drug Enforcement Administration (DEA) over narcotics violations in the United States. The expanded and coordinated effort led to the seizure of millions of dollars in controlled substances, the arrests of major narcotics figures, and the dismantling of important drug rings.

On another front, Webster strengthened the FBI's response to white-collar crimes. The Bureau investigated corruption in Congress, the judiciary, and state legislatures in California and South Carolina. The FBI also handled fraud investigations in the wake of the savings and loan collapse. This investigation grew from 10 cases in 1981 to 282 in 1987.

On May 26, 1987, Judge Webster left the FBI to become Director of the CIA. Executive Assistant Director John E. Otto became Acting Director. During his tenure, he designated drug investigations as the FBI's fifth national priority.

On November 2, 1987, former federal Judge William Steele Sessions was sworn in as FBI Director. He would lead the Bureau through a time of tremendous upheaval across the world.

In 1989, the Berlin Wall fell; the rest of the Iron Curtain soon followed. On Christmas Day 1991, the Soviet Union vanished, and the United States became the world's only superpower.

THE NINETIES

In January 1992, the FBI moved 300 Special Agents from foreign counterintelligence duties to violent crime investigations across the country. This reflected a change in national priorities and problems—including a 40 percent increase in violent crimes over the past decade.

Director Sessions expanded an FBI-Washington, DC police program that had proved successful in fighting street crime. "Operation Safe Streets" rolled out nationwide, helping law enforcement agencies across the country target fugitives and gangs in their jurisdictions.

The FBI also continued to fight "crime in the suites," or white-collar crime, including large-scale insider bank fraud and financial crimes, complex health care fraud, and newly established criminal sanctions enforcing federal environmental laws.

The Bureau expanded its definition of threats to national security, including the proliferation of chemical, biological, and nuclear weapons; the loss of critical technologies; and the improper collection of trade secrets and proprietary information.

On the domestic front, two events of the early 1990s had a major impact on FBI policies and operations.

In August 1992, Deputy U.S. Marshal William Degan was killed at Ruby Ridge, Idaho, while participating in a surveillance of federal fugitive Randall Weaver. During the resulting standoff, Weaver's wife was accidentally shot and killed by an FBI sniper.

In April 1993, outside Waco, Texas, FBI agents tried to end a 51-day standoff with members of a heavily armed religious group who had killed four officers of the Bureau of Alcohol, Tobacco, and Firearms. As agents watched in horror, fires lit by members of the group burned the compund to the ground.. Eighty people, including children, died in the blaze.

These two events provoked public outcry and congressional inquiries into the FBI's crisis response.

Director Sessions was removed from his post on July 19, 1993, following allegations of ethics violations. President Clinton appointed Deputy Director Floyd I. Clarke as Acting FBI Director. Louis J. Freeh was sworn in as Director of the FBI on September 1, 1993.

Freeh had served as an agent from 1975 to 1981 in the New York before leaving to join the U.S. Attorney's Office for the Southern District of New

York. Freeh prosecuted many major FBI cases, including the notorious "Pizza Connection" case and the "VANPAC" mail bomb case. He was appointed a U.S. District Court Judge for the Southern District of New York in 1991.

Freeh faced both deepening crime problems and a climate of government downsizing. Soon after taking office, he announced a major reorganization. Many management positions were abolished; certain divisions and offices were merged, reorganized, or eliminated; and 600 Special Agents in administrative positions were reassigned to investigative positions. Freeh also gained approval to end a two-year hiring freeze on new agents.

During his tenure, Freeh worked to develop cooperation among law enforcement agencies across the country and around the world through task forces and expanded education programs at the FBI National Academy. He also positioned the Bureau to deal with changing criminal challenges. In fact, Freeh (in conjunction with the State Department, Drug Enforcement Administration, and United States Secret Service) opened a training academy in Budapest, Hungary, in 1995 that is similar to the FBI National Academy. This academy is positioned to share expertise and develop the needed international relationships to address developing transnational criminal acts.

THE PRESENT

Freeh left the FBI in June 2001, and was succeeded by Robert S. Mueller, who was appointed by President George W. Bush on September 4, 2001. Within weeks, Mueller would be challenged by the events and attacks following September 11, 2001. Mueller, a former United States Attorney, manuevered quickly to address the demands that have drastically changed the face and mission of the FBI. Chapter 5 goes into more depth about how the attacks on the World Trade Center and the Pentagon, and the events following, affected the Bureau.

The FBI has come a long way from that first force of 34 agents. Those guys weren't even authorized to carry guns all the time; today's agents are issued guns *and* laptops. But there is one thing that has stayed the same, through almost 90 years—the motivation behind the Bureau's motto:

Fidelity, Bravery, and Integrity.

The Organizational Structure of the FBI

In official terms, the FBI is the principal investigative arm of the United States Department of Justice, assigned a four-part mission:

- Uphold the law through investigation of criminal violations
- Protect the United States from foreign intelligence and terrorist activities
- Provide leadership and law enforcement assistance to federal, state, local, and international agencies
- Perform these responsibilities in a manner that is responsive to the needs of the public and is faithful to the Constitution of the United States

The incresingly complex FBI mission always continues to grow. The latest published budget for the FBI is $4.298 billion, with over $540 million allotted to enhance technology, forensics, training, and interagency cooperation efforts.

FBI STRUCTURE

Let's take a quick view of how the FBI is organized, from headquarters to the field.

Headquarters, located on Pennsylvania Avenue in Washington, DC, is divided into four areas of services. They are:

Administration	**Law Enforcement Services**
Administrative Services Division	Critical Incident Response Group
Finance Division	Criminal Justice Information Services Division
Information Technology Operations Division	Operational Technology Division
Office of Professional Responsibility	Laboratory Division
Records Management Division	Office of Law Enforcement Coordination
Security Division	Office of International Operations
	Training and Development Division
Counterterrorism/CounterIntelligence	**Office of General Counsel**
Counterintelligence Division	Litigation Branch
Counterterrorism Division	Administrative and Technology Branch
Criminal Investigative Division	Legal Advice and Training Branch
Cyber Division	National Security Law Branch
Office of Intellligence	Hiring/Application Branch

Administration handles finance, information technology, operations, internal inquiries regarding professional behavior, records management, and the security of FBI buildings and employees.

Counterterrorism/Counterintelligence directs the efforts noted by its title, as well as criminal investigations, cybercrime, and the new Office of Intelligence.

Law Enforcement Services administers the Critical Incident Response Group, Criminal Justice Information services, investigative technology, the lab, interagency partnerships, and training and development.

The Office of General Counsel houses the lawyers handling all FBI business—the in-house counsel.

From Headquarters, the Bureau's program direction and support are fanned out to a nationwide network, with additional outposts around the world:

- 56 field offices
- Over 400 satellite offices, or Resident Agencies
- Four specialized field installations
- 45 foreign liaison posts, or Legal Attachés

Field Offices

Contact information for the 56 FBI Field Offices begins on page 265.

LEADERSHIP

The Director is supported by his staff and the Deputy Director. Each division is overseen by an Assistant Director. The offices are headed by an Inspector in Charge or General Counsel. The Assistant Directors, Inspectors in Charge, and General Counsel are supported by Deputies, Section Chiefs, Unit Chiefs, and Supervisors.

Each FBI field office is normally directed by a Special Agent in Charge (SAC), who is assisted by at least one Assistant Special Agent in Charge (ASAC). Depending on its size, each field office has one or more squads of Special Agents, managed by Supervisory Special Agents. An Office Services Manager administers support operations, such as clerical services. The largest field offices—in Los Angeles, New York City, and Washington, DC— are managed by an Assistant Director in Charge (ADIC), who is then supported by multiple SACs and ASACs.

Each of the 400 Resident Agencies is managed by a Resident Agent, or a Supervisory Resident Agent, who reports to the SAC overseeing his or her territory. The ADICs and the SACs report to the Director of the FBI, the Deputy Director, or the Assistant Directors.

Finally, the FBI also maintains four specialized field facilities. Each of these is managed by a Special Agent and professional support personnel, who report to the appropriate division or divisions at FBI Headquarters.

FBI Specialized Field Installations

- **Regional Computer Support Centers**
  These are located in Pocatello, Idaho, and Fort Monmouth, New Jersey.
- **Information Technology Centers**
  These centers in Butte, Montana, and in Savannah, Georgia, provide information services supporting investigative and administrative operations.
- **National Drug Intelligence Center**
  This center in Johnstown, Pennsylvania, collects and consolidates drug-trafficking intelligence developed by law enforcement. The NDIC receives FBI support, though it is overseen by the Department of Justice.
- **El Paso Drug Intelligence Center**
  This center combats drug trafficking. The EPDIC is run by the DEA, with FBI assistance.

In recent years, the FBI has generated a model Regional Intelligence Center in the St. Louis Division, which has resulted in very positive relationships and outcomes. This intelligence center is being considered Bureau-wide.

INTERNATIONAL OPERATIONS

It is no surprise the FBI has operational authority overseas. But the Bureau has long believed that good law enforcement doesn't stop at the United States border. The FBI maintains offices, or Legal Attachés, within the United States Embassies in over 30 countries around the world. Each Legal Attaché, or "Legat," is headed by a Special Agent with the title of Legal Attaché, supported by one or more Assistant Legal Attachés. The Bureau also operates three Liaison Offices in Honolulu, Hawaii, Miami, Florida, and San Juan, Puerto Rico. Special Agents, or Liaison Officers, cover designated areas of the Pacific Rim and the Caribbean, and maintain contact with the law enforcement and intelligence services in foreign countries within their jurisdictions.The FBI has since opened offices in Russia, Estonia, Lithuania, Latvia, and other emerging Soviet independant states. Assignments overseas are no longer considered unusual.

FBI Special Agents generally don't have arrest authority outside the United States. However, arrests can be made under treaty agreements with agents involved. Since the Legats exist for liaison purposes, Legal Attachés and Liaison Officers are not granted law enforcement powers in foreign countries.

The FBI's Role in Society

The FBI's investigative authority is the broadest of all federal law enforcement agencies. The Bureau is responsible for all criminal violations that aren't specifically assigned to another agency, as well as those in specific areas assigned by Congress, the President, or the Attorney General.

The FBI does not work in a vacuum, and clearly must develop and nurture relationships with other police agencies, as well as with the public. In recent years, there has been an increasing interest in the element of information/ intelligence sharing. You've heard "information is power?" Power today is based on the ability to see beyond the parochialism of the past and to view the country's problems as shared by all. Each level of law enforcment brings its own expertise to these situations. Professional respect is the foundation of the relationships between agencies.

But things don't change overnight. Many agencies, not unlike the FBI, have acted autonomously for many, many years. Stereotypes are often hard to overcome, but a new generation of law enforcement is increasingly successful in this regard.

AN AGENT'S ROLE

What is the magic? Let's consider a Special Agent's preparation and role before we proceed to specialty positions and assignments. As an Agent recruit, you attend a 15-week training course at Quantico, Virginia, upon appointment to the FBI. Then you arrive in Washington DC, take the oath of office at FBI headquarters, and report to the Academy. You then spend the next several weeks training physically and becoming familiar with the skills required of an agent, the law, firearm use, and practical scenarios. Remember, though, the Academy is only the beginning of the extensive education you will receive over a career both in a classroom and in the field. The FBI's greatest strength is its camraderie—it is a source of great personal satisfaction, and is extremely integral to the solution of complex investigative matters. This camraderie operates across positional lines, with all FBI employees working as a unit toward the mission.

So, midway during your training you will receive notification of your first division assignment. This is when it all becomes real. You will begin communicating with your assigned office regarding your reporting date and first squad assignment. The feeling of FBI family starts early—while still in the Academy, you may receive assistance finding housing, schools, and other details necessary to your upcoming transition.

After graduation from the Academy, you report to your Office of Assignment and are assigned to a squad. This is a time in your career to keep your mouth shut and learn. Working cases and becoming familiar with office operations and personnel will make your transition easier. In the culture of the FBI and other police agencies, it is important to "pay your dues" and learn case work—from the most tedious assignments to the more exciting. Try to remember, cases come and go, but relationships do not. That may be difficult for new agents who may have left important corporate positions or for those in the military who commanded many operations. But remember, you will integrate your talents and earn the fast respect of colleagues with a cooperative attitude.

You may be assigned cases that you can readily address with the assistance or input of more senior personnel. Become familiar with the Administrative Services dimension of the office, and create positive relations here. Administrative Services handles evidence storage, technical assistance, record management, vehicle purchase, outfitting and maintenance, expert computer support, and anything else you require to accomplish your duties. Many of these employees have advanced degrees or training, and invesitgative analysts and other specialists are assigned to specific squads. Personnel assigned to this side of the house are inextricably tied to the success of all cases.

Each office you are assigned to will have a different personality depending on its regional location, size, and the type of work conducted at the city headquarters and in Resident Agencies. For example, many of the Southwest and Northwest Divisions handle the unique work of Indian Country criminal matters. In these offices, working on these matters requires maturity, independence, and creativity. You will be working closely with Bureau of Indian Affairs' Agents and Tribal Police. These assignments entail long hours and intense casework involving violent personal crimes. If assigned to one of the Illinois Divisions you will find that 95% of the work is in Resident Agencies located in major university cities and rural communities. Each assignment offers very different challenges.

One of the greatest aspects of working for the FBI is the range of diversity in assignments and the ability to avail yourself of specialized training. Once you have established yourself as a knowledgeable "street agent," there are opportunities to work varied "Specials" (individually directed work assignment often outside of your home division): undercover assignments, technical assignments, Surveillance Teams, Special Weapons and Tactical Teams, Hostage Rescue Teams, Evidence Response Teams, and major case assignments requiring an influx of personnel. You are able to receive specialized training from FBI Academy Inservices, FBI Regional Training events, business or specialized corporate training, United States

Department of Defense Language School, and often military Hazardous Materials training or Bomb Detection and Response.

In a career with the FBI, you can pursue personal excellence down many paths. You may dedicate yourself to a particular crime problem. You may seek expertise in the sciences and go back to the Laboratory or teach at the Academy. You may wish to become involved in Police Training both here or overseas. Within any of these options are several branches of expertise.

The Evidence Response teams are relatively new, and many of these specialized teams travel overseas where needed. Agents have been sent to Rihad, Saudia Arabia, regarding bombings of a U.S. military installation and personnel. The bombings of U.S. Embassies in Nigeria and Tanzania and the pursuit of Taliban or Al Queda targets in Pakistan and Afghanistan are the most notable cases where specialized personnel have been sent abroad. Traveling teams are no longer the exception, but the rule.

And this is only the agent's position. Many Support Personnel operate all over the country and world, as well, providing important contributions to investigations; analysts, language specialists, special surveillance groups (SSG), and Rapid Start information processing teams are invaluable in assisting large scale investigations.

Running investigations and working together on major cases is the meat of a job with the FBI. You will be working with police from all levels of government and from throughout the world. You will represent the FBI in these situations.

WHAT THE FBI ISN'T

Historically, people get confused about the difference between the FBI and all the other federal agencies associated with law enforcement or investigations of various kinds. Agents often get asked what it's like to guard the President. The answer is "no idea." However, FBI agents do participate in protection details often involving U.S. government officials and foreign dignitaries.

Take the FBI in relation to the CIA. The CIA actually has no law enforcement function. The CIA collects and analyzes information needed to develop U.S. policy, especially security policy. The CIA is authorized to gather information on foreign countries and their citizens exclusively; it is specifically prohibited from collecting information concerning "U.S. persons"—a legal term that includes U.S. citizens, resident aliens, legal immigrants, and U.S. corporations, regardless of where they are located. On the other hand, the FBI is entirely about investigating crimes among and directed at "U.S. persons." Given the circumstances of post-September 11, accountability and redirection of personnel and resources will continue to occur as a result of Congressional investigations.

Two other federal agencies involved with law enforcement—the Drug Enforcement Agency (DEA) and the Bureau of Alcohol Tobacco and Firearms (BATF)—are often confused with the FBI. Here are the differences: While the FBI is charged with enforcement of over 300 federal violations, the DEA is a single-mission agency dealing solely with enforcement of drug laws. The BATF also has a relatively restricted area of investigation—its major responsibility is enforcing federal firearms statutes and investigating arsons and bombings that aren't related to terrorism.

Obviously, the aims of the Bureau and these other agencies often overlap. The FBI always stresses cooperation and coordination, not competition. The FBI works with all these agencies on specific cases and ongoing task forces.

WORKING TOGETHER

I have found that forging relationships with other agency personnel only improved me as an FBI agent. Your versatility and liaison capabilities will be an important mark of the FBI's success. I've mentioned over and over how much the FBI stresses cooperation among law enforcement agencies, and that's absolutely true. The FBI doesn't "take over" investigations from state or local police. State and local law enforcement agencies aren't subordinate to the FBI, and the FBI doesn't supervise or usurp their investigations.

Here's how Bob McGonigel puts it: "I've worked with police departments all over the country, and it was a great experience for me. We complemented each other. I was aware of people's sensitivities, and I'd try to put them at ease and let them know that I'm just there to do the job. Don't want my picture taken, and don't want the credit. I just want to work toward a solution of the case. Once they realize that, they put away those petty differences. I was never one who was opposed to learning a more effective way, or a more sensible way to do it. I don't have all the answers."

Each agency brings an expertise to the table. However, the FBI does have resources and experience most other law enforcement agencies can't match. The Bureau strengthens the fight against crime on all levels by providing these resources to efforts being confronted by multiple agencies.

For instance, the FBI's centralized information databases help apprehend fugitives. When local agencies report a fugitive to the Bureau, a stop is placed against the fugitive's fingerprints in the FBI's Criminal Justice Information Services Division. If any additional fingerprints are turned into the FBI, local police will be notified immediately. The fugitive's name and identifying data also will be entered into the National Crime Information Center, a computerized database that is accessible to law enforcement agencies nationwide. Any agency requesting information about this individual will be informed of his or her fugitive status. If there is reason to believe a fugitive has traveled across a state line or left the United States, the FBI may obtain a federal arrest warrant and join the investigation.

Through the National Name Check Program, specific information from the FBI's central records system is made available to other entities lawfully authorized to receive it—other federal agencies in the Executive Branch, congressional committees, the federal judiciary, some foreign police and intelligence agencies, and state and local agencies within the criminal justice system. The individual's rights are safeguarded, as well; information is released only in accordance with the provisions of the federal Privacy Act, and other applicable federal orders and directives.

One of the FBI's most effective cooperative means of fighting criminal activity is through its range of multiagency task forces. Since the 1970s, the use of task forces has been a successful tool for interagency cooperation. If employed by the FBI, you may be assigned to the varied task forces in which the FBI participates:

- Drug Task Forces
- Organized Crime Task Forces
- Bank Robbery Task Forces
- Terrorism Task Forces
- Fugitive Task Forces
- Cybercrime Task Forces
- Child Pornogrpahy Task Forces
- Safe Streets Task Forces (urban)
- Safe Trails Task Forces (Indian country)

These have proven to be a very effective way for the FBI and state and local law enforcement to join together to address specific crime problems. Criminals generally don't pay a lot of attention to jurisdictional matters— a crime may be a local, state, and federal violation all at the same time. Task forces organize the law enforcement response and represent the best use of scarce resources.

Here are only a few of the vital resources the FBI has to offer in such joint ventures.

Evidence Response Team (ERT)

Each FBI field office supports an ERT, which specializes in recovery of physical evidence and the execution of search warrants. The ERTs are called out in cases with complicated or multiple crime scenes, in multijurisdictional cases, and in cases requiring the most sophisticated forensic analyses. Seventeen ERTs from across the country participated in evidence recovery at the bombing of the Oklahoma City federal building and the bombings overseas in Naroibi and Saudi Arabia, as well as the disaster scenes of September 11, 2001. The Oklahoma Bombing resulted in a 100 percent increase in call-outs for ERTs. In 2002, 135 ERTs responded to over 2,000 incidents. In fact, after 9/11, 52 ERTs of over 400 members worked for nine months in response to the attacks. ERTs also train local and international police in evidence recovery procedures, as the New York ERT (NY/ERT) recently did in Paraguay.

The 36–member NY/ERT is one of the most active teams in the country, providing most of the New York Office's forensic capability. Participating in the task force is strictly voluntary; everyone on the team has to balance training and operational requirements with everyday squad duties. And these people do work hard. The NY/ERT—and all members of special task forces—put pressure on themselves to make sure their operational, training, and administrative standards are not only met, but improved upon.

A coordinator heads up the three NY/ERT teams—Red, White, and Blue. Each 12-person team rotates "on duty" status every two weeks. In the case of a major disaster, such as TWA 800 or 9/11, everyone on the task force is called out.

Staff Duties

The coordinator serves as the overall program manager, with other team members handling organizational responsibilities:

- The Operations/Training Officer coordinates the training activities, researches new training programs, and acts as the NY/ERT's liaison with the FBI and outside agencies.

- The Equipment/Logistics Officer maintains adequate supplies for operational missions, keeps records of equipment issued to each ERT member, and coordinates logistical support for the NY/ERT during missions outside the team's jurisdiction.
- The Medical Officer coordinates medical training, keeps on top of members' inoculations, and makes sure any injuries are documented and referred to the Health Services Unit.
- The Team Leader communicates training and operation requirements to the team and keeps track of the day-to-day availability and accountability of team members.
- The Assistant Team Leader steps in as the Team Leader in his or her absence, and performs major assignments as directed by the Team leader.
- The Administrative Officer maintains accurate and current records on team personnel and administration.

Equipment

Besides the usual equipment any crime scene unit would have—evidence vacuums, latent fingerprinting equipment, laptop computers, alternative light sources—the NY/ERT operates two vehicles outfitted with emergency light package and state-of-the-art communications equipment. These vehicles can operate over radio frequencies in the VHF and UHF range, issue secure communications via cellular telephone, and provide AC power in the field.

The NY/ERT also operates two full-size heavy equipment trucks, a cargo van, and a step van; these are used as needed in major-response situations and for supply purposes. A 14-foot trailer is used in the New York region to transport bulky, specialized equipment not needed on most responses. An 18-foot trailer is stocked with supplies and equipment needed when the team deploys to a major event nationally, or even internationally; this trailer can keep two ERT teams supplied for three days.

Training

Evidence recovery is crucial to the successful investigation and prosecution of a crime. The highly trained Special Agent and support personnel who make up an ERT specialize in organizing and collecting evidence using a variety of technical evidence recovery techniques. ERTs also include personnel with specialized forensic training and unique collection abilities; these skills prove invaluable in unusual searches or crime scenes.

The NY/ERT conducts regular training sessions. Each team member also completes at least 80 hours of basic instruction provided by the FBI's Evidence Response Team Unit (ERTU). The NY/ERT aggressively searches out training opportunities from sources outside the Bureau. And the NY/ERT, along with all the ERTs, establishes partnerships in the law enforcement community to obtain and provide training and operational support wherever needed. The Chicago/ERT has trained with highly specialized military Hazardous Materials Units through the extraordinary liaison efforts of its team.

Safe Streets

This task force targets violent crime and drug trafficking in areas where state or local authorities have identified it as a significant local concern. Participating law enforcement officers work closely with Special Agents at the relevant Field Offices, and receive intensive training in dealing with the specific problems they are likely to face on the streets. As of March 2000, 174 Safe Streets Task Forces had been established in 54 field offices. These task forces include 1,096 state and local officers, 805 FBI Agents, and 251 persons from other federal agencies. Since 1992, over 100,000 criminals have been arrested under the Safe Streets program.

Two Very Special Agents

One of the difficulties of working for the FBI is achieving balance in your life—not letting the job take over. I think we can learn a few lessons in this area from a couple of members of the NY/ERT. These two guys focus completely on the task when they are at work, devoting every ounce of their energy and concentration to the job. But when they are off-duty, they are off. They don't worry about what they should have done last time, or what they might do next time. They give it all they've got, and then they move on. Instead of reacting to stress by boozing it up or snarling at the kids, they just chew on a rawhide and take a nap.

I'm talking, of course, about the canine component of the New York K-9 Program, part of the NY/ERT.

Axel was born in June 1994, of mixed parentage—Rottweiler and German shepherd. He's very well educated; he completed a 400-hour narcotics detection course at the New Jersey State Police Canine Academy. He's certified to detect heroin, cocaine, crack, hashish, marijuana, and metham-phetamines; when he sniffs out any of these substances, he scratches and bites at the spot where the odor is strongest. During training, he conduct-ed 160 successful searches at a range of locations—cars, helicopters, boats, trucks, buses, houses, apartments, warehouses, institutions, and open fields. Since starting work for the FBI, he's partici-pated in searches which have resulted in the seizure of over 324.73 kilos of cocaine, 859 grams of crack cocaine, and 361 grams of marijuana, all with an estimated street value of $7,162,290.

Jake is a four-year-old black Labrador Retriever whose specialty is explo-sive chemical detection. His training, which began at six months, included basic obedience and introduction to explosive residues. He's trained to give a passive response when he detects explosives—biting and scratching could set off the explosives, so instead Jake just sits down. He's been credited with recovery of firearms, fireworks, explosives. He and his handler, a Special Agent bomb technician, assisted in TWA 800 recovery efforts.

Rapid Start Team

Any law enforcement official knows that the first hours—even the first minutes—of a crime investigation can make or break its success. The FBI's Rapid Start Team allows law enforcement to establish and maintain control of complicated cases from the very beginning.

Under Rapid Start, FBI Special Agents and support personnel provide on-site automation for major cases and crises. In the event of a murder, kidnapping, or other task force case, a Rapid Start Team travels to the jurisdiction and works with local officials to organize and enter all pertinent facts into one database. The information can then be sorted, filtered, and analyzed instantaneously. This allows for effective lead management, and helps investigators quickly identify the most productive investigative approaches. The Rapid Start Team has been responsible for operating in many investigations, including the 1993 bombing of the World Trade Center and the subsequent 9/11 attacks.

Critical Incident Response Group (CIRG)

This unit was formed to address hostage-taking, barricade situations, terrorist activities, and other critical incidents requiring an emergency response by diverse law enforcement resources. CIRG provides training and operational support in crisis management, negotiations, criminal profiling, and special weapons and tactics (SWAT).

SWAT Teams

Nine enhanced SWAT teams are strategically located throughout the United States. They are called into action in the most critical and dangerous situations.

Special Agent Phil Grivas was on SWAT teams for 17 years, and spent six years as a SWAT team commander. He describes this experience: "You can't imagine what it's like to give people an order to go into a situation, knowing that they may not be coming back. It's one thing to go through the door yourself. I never gave it a second thought. But when you're in charge of the team, they become like your kids. You get protective of them.

"When you have to send other people through the front door, that's when you really hope and pray that your plan covers everything. The selection of personnel, the equipment, the weaponry, the communications, all of it—you have to plan and drill and plan and drill some more, to minimize the chance of any more people getting hurt. I've got a lot to be grateful for in my career, and one of the biggest things is the fact that I left without any of my people getting hurt."

Hostage Rescue Team (HRT)

The HRT was created in 1982 as a special counterterrorist unit, offering a tactical option for any extraordinary hostage crisis that might occur within the United States. The team is set up to deploy to any location within four hours of notification by the Director of the FBI or his designated representative. Once there, the team's mission is to conduct a successful rescue of U.S. persons and others who may be held illegally by a hostile force. Team members specialize in communication, command control, use of sophisticated electronic equipment, and handling of explosive devices.

The HRT has been deployed to the scenes of such incidents as prison riots in Georgia and Alabama, the "Freemen" standoff in Jordan, Montana, the bombing at the 1996 Summer Olympics in Atlanta, Georgia, and the U.S. embassy bombing overseas in the late 90s.

Profiling and Behavioral Assessment Unit (PBAU)

I wish there were no need for this unit. This group helps investigate the most brutal, most violent crimes, including child abductions, serial murders, and serial sex crimes. Unfortunately, there has been an increase in all these crimes over the past 20 years. These cases are not only heartbreaking, but they are also complicated and extremely difficult to solve. Investigations of this kind require an immediate all-out response, and a long-term commitment of more personnel and resources than many police departments can spare.

PBAU's primary responsibility is to provide immediate investigative support through violent crime analysis, technical and forensic resource coordination, and application of the most current expertise available. While most cops will never investigate serial killings, mass murders, abductions, or mysterious disappearances, PBAU deals with these kinds of crimes all the time. The members of this unit can draw on years of experience in assessing leads, developing strategies, and evaluating evidence. That saves time, which often means saving lives.

The goal is always to support the investigative agencies in first recovering the victim or victims and then fully resolving the case—ideally, through a conviction.

PBAU Special Agents provide the following services:

- Profiles of unknown subjects (UNSUBs)
- Crime analysis
- Investigative strategies
- Interview and interrogation strategies
- Trial preparation and prosecution strategy
- Expert testimony
- Coordination of other FBI resources, including the use of the Evidence Response Team, Laboratory services, and Rapid Start

PBAU also maintains a close working relationship with the National Center for Missing and Exploited Children, and can help in arranging use of their resources, such as widespread poster distribution and age enhancement of photographs.

The Violent Criminal Apprehension Program, (VICAP), a part of the PBAU, is designed to collect, collate, and analyze the aspects of violent crimes so that through computer analysis and data processing, violent crimes can be compared, identified, and charted. In addition, experienced Major Case Specialists and Crime Analysts review the violent crime cases submitted and are able to provide their investigative and analytical expertise to the submitting law enforcement agencies. Through this process, suspects can be identified, crimes can be linked, and widespread law enforcement agencies can combine their resources to focus on a common criminal.

National Center for the Analysis of Violent Crime (NCAVC)

One of my personal obsessions has been the development of a nationwide resource for fighting particularly vicious crimes. Without a way for law enforcement agencies to compare notes, the most violent, most predatory criminals can escape capture by simply moving from one jurisdiction to another. A killer or rapist vanishes once he leaves the first area, and then appears from nowhere when he begins his crimes somewhere new.

In 1985, NCAVC was formed to combat this problem. Based at the National Academy, NCAVC offers research, training, and investigative and operational support to law enforcement agencies across the country confronted with unusual, high-risk, vicious, or repetitive crimes. Research activities include the study of serial and violent crimes (such as homicide, rape, child abduction, arson, threats, and computer crimes) as well as hijacking, crisis management, and subjects related to hostage negotiation and SWAT team operations. Investigative support is also offered through VICAP to alert law enforcement agencies that may be seeking the same offender for crimes in different jurisdictions.

Regional Drug Intelligence Squads (RDIs)

These multiagency information-gathering groups are based in eight geographic regions—all identified as key trans-shipment centers for illegal drugs. Intelligence information uncovered by RDIs often triggers major drug investigations. Using the Racketeering Enterprise Investigation concept, team members focus on getting information about the most serious drug-trafficking organizations operating in their areas—including their composition, scope, magnitude, internal and external dynamics, and drug-trafficking patterns. Once collected, this information is analyzed and provided to the federal, state, or local law enforcement agency best suited to handle the case.

DRUGX

This joint FBI-DEA drug index database became operational in 1995. It merges over 4.4 million FBI drug records (culled from case index information) with more than 4.1 million DEA records. When the FBI considers opening an investigation on a subject, it can first check to see if the DEA has an investigation on the same subject (or vice versa). This preliminary check saves valuable resources and man-hours by reducing duplicate efforts.

National Drug Intelligence Center (NDIC)

NDIC was established in 1993 to provide a strategic picture of drug-distribution organizations as they evolve in response to the market and law-enforcement efforts. Participating agencies include the FBI and the DEA, along with other federal law enforcement, intelligence and military agencies. NDIC analysts gather information from the field and from the participating agencies' headquarters, then prepare reports, studies, and other research on requested topics.

The NDIC is in the process of developing an electronic library which would enable participating agencies to research specific topics. These services should eventually be available to state and local law enforcement as well.

El Paso Intelligence Center (EPIC)

This multiagency, 24-hour electronic monitoring post keeps tabs on drug trafficking organizations operating across the U.S./Mexico border. EPIC's primary focus is on drug-trafficking activities in the Southwest, but EPIC investigators and analysts from the 15 or so participating agencies also collect and analyze tactical drug intelligence from other areas—including foreign countries—whose drug activities impact on the United States. EPIC also prepares periodic assessments of the threat posed by drug-trafficking organizations worldwide. EPIC also acts as an information clearinghouse, regularly sharing automated drug data among participating agencies. This results in better coordinated, more effective investigations.

International Activities

In the course of their operations, the FBI's Legal Attaché Offices sometimes receive information relevant to FBI organized crime and drug cases in the United States and pass on certain information that may help the law enforcement agencies with jurisdiction in the region. The FBI has over 50 offices in 26 nations worldwide. In the last several years, the workload of these offices tops over 20,000 investigative matters per year.

The FBI regularly participates in international working groups with countries including Italy, Australia, Canada, and Mexico. The Bureau also exchanges midlevel supervisory personnel with police agencies in countries such as Germany, Italy, Australia, and Japan, and with INTERPOL. This regular and ongoing linkage facilitates a rapid exchange of information on drug smuggling and other international crimes.

Since the dissolution of the Soviet Union, the FBI has established Legat Offices in many of these emerging states. These liaison efforts were instrumental following the September 11 attacks, as our interest focused on both Pakistan and Afghanistan. Former Director Louis J. Freeh envisioned the need for these relationships as the world's interest in law enforcment and state matters increased.

137

DNA Technology

In 1993, DNA technology was recognized by courts as viable and accepted evidence. The FBI has increased the credibility of the lab by placing a scientist to oversee its operation. The FBI Laboratory, with its extensive technical resources and expertise, has become a world leader in the forensic use of DNA. Currently, the FBI's work with DNA is focused in two areas:

- FBI laboratories now use new DNA casework tests based on a technique for amplifying small quantities of genetic material. This means that the tests can be effective and meaningful, even with there's only a tiny sample of blood or other material available—which is often the case with crime scene evidence.
- The new Combined DNA Index System (CODIS) is a database containing DNA profiles of convicted sex offenders and other violent offenders, as well as missing persons. CODIS allows state and local crime labs to match DNA profiles from UNSUBs in serial rape cases with unknown suspects, helping refocus investigative efforts. When it is deployed nationwide, CODIS will allow law enforcement to review all 20,000 convicted offender DNA records held in 45 DNA crime labs across the country.

History of Fingerprinting

Back in the 1880s, when a criminal was arrested, he wasn't fingerprinted. He was measured—more carefully and more thoroughly than a guy being fitted for a custom-made suit—according to the principles of the Bertillon method.

Alphonse Bertillon, a French police officer, is considered the father of forensics. In the late 1800s, he developed an elaborate identification system based on 243 body measurements, including height, arm span, length of the torso, and length of the right ear. Sounds wacky now, but this was a time when "doctors of phrenology" claimed to analyze your character by feeling the bumps on your head.

The Bertillon method was the first attempt to apply scientific principles and techniques, such as measurement, to the job of criminal investigation—which is the foundation of forensics. But there were serious practical problems with Bertillon's system. The large number of measurements made record keeping and cross-comparison (especially in that precomputer era) very tedious and time-consuming; police often weren't as precise with their measurements as the system demanded; ambitious criminals had the bad habit of beginning their careers before they'd finished growing and their measurements had stabilized. And despite the unwieldy number of figures, a Bertillon profile wasn't unique; investigators soon discovered that more than one person could fit one profile.

At the same time Bertillon was developing his system, fingerprints were becoming more accepted as a means of identification. One of the pioneers of fingerprinting was Sir William Herschel, a British chief magistrate in Jungipoor, India. In July 1858, he started requiring the locals to put a handprint on the back of contracts, as a way of discouraging them from denying their signature later. According to the New York State Division of Criminal Justice Services (DCJS), the system accomplished its goal—not because the Indians believed in the effectiveness of the identification, but because personal contact with the document made the contract more binding. A superstitious beginning for a forensics technique, but it worked.

In the 1870s, a countryman of Herschel's developed a comprehensive system of categorizing fingerprints. Again according to DCJS, Dr. Henry Faulds, surgeon-superintendent of a hospital in Tokyo, began studying what he called "skin-furrows" after he found impressions of them in old Japanese pottery. He knew his system of classifying and comparing fingerprints could be useful in many scientific areas, especially identification. He offered his data to Scotland Yard, but they weren't interested; in 1880, Faulds sent a description of his system to the leading scientist of the day, Charles Darwin.

Darwin, old and ill by then, forwarded the information to his cousin and fellow scientific researcher, Sir Francis Galton. Galton didn't take up the project until 1888, when the Royal Institute invited him to give a lecture on personal identification.

Galton planned to focus on the Bertillon method, but "wishing to treat the subject generally, and having a vague knowledge of the value sometimes assigned to finger marks," Galton also started researching this new-fangled technique, beginning with data collected by Faulds and Herschel.

At first, Galton believed fingerprints might offer a way to trace heredity and racial background—a particular interest of that era. But Galton soon realized that the real value of fingerprints lay in their possibilities for identification. As both Faulds and Herschel had suspected, a person's fingerprints were both unique and permanent. Unless deliberately erased or altered, they remained the same throughout a lifetime.

Galton identified three basic classifications of fingerprints: loops, which bend back on themselves like a loop of string; whorls, or tiny spirals; and arches, anything that isn't a loop or a whorl. Galton's system assigned a numerical position to each fingertip and then classified the general characteristics of each fingertip; this created a ten-letter sequence that was easily recorded, easily compared, and almost infallible. (Galton's system has since been updated and simplified, but the loops, whorls, and arches terminology is still used.)

Dr. Faulds accused Galton of plagiarizing his own system, and the two recording methods are remarkably similar. But Galton remains the official originator of fingerprinting.

For the rest of the nineteenth century, fingerprinting and Bertillonage coexisted as state-of-the-art identification techniques, but the practical benefits of fingerprinting soon won out. During the 1900s, police departments in almost every major metropolitan city in the United States converted to fingerprinting. Some departments, such as New York State's, sent representatives to Scotland Yard to pick the brains of the experts—an early example of international cooperation between law enforcement agencies.

In 1905, the Department of Justice created a Bureau of Criminal Identification (BCI) to provide a centralized archive of fingerprint cards. Two years later, the collection was moved to Kansas to take advantage of a large supply of cheap labor—convicts at Leavenworth Federal Penitentiary.

Understandably enough, police officers were dubious about this misguided effort to save money. They formed their own centralized bureau, which flat out refused to share data with the BCI.

In 1924, Congress merged the two collections and put them under Bureau of Investigation administration. By 1926, law enforcement agencies across the country were contributing fingerprint cards to the Bureau of Investigation. The FBI's identification division soon became, and remains, the most comprehensive archive in the country.

National Crime Information Center (NCIC)

NCIC was established in 1967 as a nationwide computerized information system to provide law enforcement with information on fugitives, stolen property, and other information. The enhanced system incorporates advanced technologies such as capture, transmission, retrieval, and print-out of fugitives' photographs and fingerprint images, as well as other improvements.

SELECTED CASE DISCUSSIONS

To help you understand how all of these resources are utilized, let's look at a few FBI joint venture investigations from selected categories:

Civil Rights Program

The FBI investigates all violations of federal civil rights statutes; the Department of Justice determines prosecution. Civil rights violations, often referred to as Hate Crimes, fall into several categories:

- Racial or religious discrimination
- Abuses "under color of law"—use of excessive force or police misconduct
- Involuntary servitude or slavery
- Violation of the Voting Rights Act of 1965
- Violation of the Civil Rights Act of 1964
- Violation of the Equal Credit Opportunity Act
- Violation of the Freedom of Access to Clinic Entrances Act
- Violation of the Civil Rights of Institutionalized Persons Act

Hate crime violations investigated by the FBI involve cases of injury or death allegedly caused by the use of excessive force by law enforcement officers or by individuals adverse to citizens of different races, gender identifications, or sexual preferences. For example, every year the FBI investigates hundreds of cases regarding police brutality; on average, about 30 law enforcement personnel are eventually convicted. Most police departments go to great lengths, as the FBI does, in recruiting good people. No system is perfect. The FBI leads investigations of racial violence, homicides, verbal or written threats, and the desecration of property. As Morris Dees (social justice lawyer and activist) calls it, the "gathering storm" of vigilante militias presents a new and threatening crime problem in the United States. The FBI was involved in those investigations as the Oklahoma Bombing matter unfolded and the Michigan militia came to the attention of the public.

The Silent Brotherhood

One of the biggest civil rights cases in recent years involved a man who was murdered because of what he said on the radio.

> Just before midnight on June 18, 1984, a quiet residential neighborhood in Denver, Colorado, was disrupted by an unfamiliar sound— a barrage of gunfire.
>
> The target was controversial radio talk show host Alan Berg. He was found in his driveway, sprawled in a pool of blood. He'd been killed instantly by shots to the head and neck. He hadn't even had time to step all the way out of his car.
>
> Berg, who called himself "the last angry man," had helped originate "shock radio." Long before Howard Stern made it big, Berg developed an abrasive style—delivering opinionated diatribes, interrupting callers, insulting and attacking them on the air. Berg's defenders

argued that he never indulged in personal attacks, but instead criticized callers' views, challenging their thinking. Still, Berg had received several death threats, including one a few months before his murder.

Denver police focused immediately on right-wing extremists; Berg's liberal viewpoints and abrasive style had led to run-ins with them before. In 1979, a Ku Klux Klan member burst into the studio while Berg was on the air. Berg said the man had threatened him with a gun. The man denied it, and the issue was later settled out of court.

Over the weeks and months following Berg's murder, Denver police questioned over 200 people and tracked down countless leads. They were sure that right-wing extremists were involved, but they couldn't get any hard evidence.

Then came the shoot-out in Sandpoint, Idaho.

During the early '80s, FBI agents in the northwestern United States came to realize that a group of antigovernment white supremacists had set up operations in the area. The group called themselves the Aryan Nation, and they were suspected of several crimes in the region, including a series of robberies. The agents identified as many of the members of the Aryan Nation as they could, and kept them under surveillance. Slowly, the agents uncovered evidence of an armed and violent group allied with the Aryan Nation—the Order, or the Silent Brotherhood. Agents began keeping track of members of the Silent Brotherhood, as well.

On October 18, 1984, three FBI agents drove down a rutted, rural driveway in Sandpoint, Idaho. They were on their way to visit Gary Lee Yarbrough, known to be a member of the Aryan Nation. Yarbrough also had links to the Order.

Before the Agents reached his house, Yarbrough opened fire. No one was injured in the resulting shoot-out, but Yarbrough escaped. The FBI Agents searched his house and found a cache of explosives and weapons, including a Mac 10 submachine gun—the same kind of gun used to kill Alan Berg. Ballistics tests proved that it was the murder weapon, and investigators had their first major break. (They later found out that Yarbrough wasn't the trigger man. The leader of the Silent Brotherhood had given Yarbrough the Mac 10 and told him to get rid of the weapon by throwing it into one of the thousands of remote mountain lakes in the region. But Yarbrough was too enamored of his new toy, and just couldn't give it up.)

Eventually, the Berg murder became one of a string of major crimes tied to the Order. The group planned an armed overthrow of the U.S. government, a project they knew would be expensive. Their money-making endeavors included counterfeiting and armed robbery, notably a $3.6 million holdup of a Brink's armored car. The Order targeted several prominent people for assassination, including television producer Norman Lear, civil rights lawyer Morris Dees, and Berg.

The FBI's extensive intelligence on right-wing extremist groups proved vital to investigating and prosecuting the case. The Aryan Nation leadership had issued death threats against a former member turned FBI informant; the man's picture and last known address were posted on the Aryan Liberty Network Website and printed in newsletters, along with threats to "remove his head from his body."

A security officer for the Aryan Nation paid $1,800 for proof of the informant's death—a photograph of the man's decapitated body. The photograph actually was a convincing fake produced in the FBI Lab, and the security officer was arrested for conspiring to kill a government witness.

In September 1985, ten members of the Order were brought to trial in Seattle, Washington, charged under the federal law against conspiring to operate a criminal enterprise. All ten were convicted, and six of the ten were also convicted of separate criminal counts. The prosecution depended on circumstantial evidence—such as hotel, telephone, and airline records—as well as expert fingerprint and ballistics testimony gathered and developed by the FBI. Most of the defendants didn't even try to shake the FBI experts' testimony.

Just over two years later, in October 1997, four members of the Order were brought to trial on federal civil rights charges in Berg's murder. The Denver district attorney declined to file murder charges, saying the circumstantial evidence didn't show a strong enough link to the defendants.

More than 80 witnesses testified in the trial, including the FBI fingerprint and ballistics experts who had testified in the racketeering trial. Bruce Pierce was accused of shooting Berg; in his opening statement, Pierce's attorney said, accurately, "There are no eyewitnesses linking him to the scene of the crime, no physical evidence linking him to the scene of the crime." But FBI witnesses linked Pierce to the murder through a fingerprint on a Denver hotel registration and ballistics tests on shells found in a house Pierce rented after Berg's death.

Two of the defendants, Pierce and the getaway driver, were convicted. U.S. District Court Judge Richard Matsch sentenced the two to serve 150 years in prison, on top of their earlier sentences for racketeering. The 150-year

sentence requires them to serve at least 50
years before they're eligible for parole. "A
life sentence would not be sufficient in this
case," Matsch said; a life sentence would have
made them eligible for parole sooner. (If
Matsch's name seems familiar, there's a reason
why. He presided over Timothy McVeigh's trial
for the Oklahoma City bombing. That may not be
the only link between the two cases. According
to some reports, McVeigh closely followed the
racketeering and civil rights trials of the
Order members.)

The investigation of The Order stretched
across most of the western United States; the
prosecution lacked eyewitness testimony and
needed convincing forensic evidence. It's
exactly this kind of complicated case that the
FBI was developed to handle.

Counterterrorism Program

The FBI is the federal agency charged with protecting the United States and
its citizens from the threat of terrorism. Since September 11, 2001, the FBI
has reoriented an entire agency's priority around foreign counterintelligence and counterterrorism. Thousands of agents, as well as budget and
resources, have been reassigned to this priority. This really is a new era for
the FBI and its personnel.

Countering terrorism effectively requires the exchange of information and
close, daily coordination among U.S. law enforcement, intelligence, and service entities. Also, the overall success in combating international terrorism

is directly attributable to a growth of international intelligence sharing and increased international law enforcement efforts.

President George W. Bush has appointed John D. Negroponte as the new National Intelligence Director. Negroponte will oversee intelligence product of over 15 intelligence agencies, including the FBI.

Generally, the FBI's counterterrorism activities fall into the following categories:

- Domestic terrorism
- Hostage taking
- Overseas homicide and attempted homicide, when the victim(s) are "U.S. persons"
- Protection of foreign officials and guests
- Sabotage
- Domestic security
- Attempted or actual bombings, when the motive is terrorism
- Nuclear extortion
- Sedition, or fostering violent rebellion against the government

Antiterrorism investigations most often involve bombings. When a bombing or bomb threat occurs, either the BATF or the FBI will be given control of the investigation. In general, the BATF investigates violations of the Federal Bombing Statute; however, Department of Justice guidelines give the FBI jurisdiction over separate violations, which the FBI handled before enactment of the Statute.

The FBI's responsibilities cover the deliberate, malicious damage or destruction of property used in interstate or foreign commerce by use of an explosive. This includes the bombing or attempted bombing of college or university facilities and incidents that seem to be the work of terrorist or revolutionary groups. Overseas, the FBI investigates bombings that are an act of terrorism against U.S. persons or interests.

Another common category of the FBI's antiterrorism work is the investigation of domestic hate groups, such as The Order. The Bureau's responsibilities in this area are outlined by the Attorney General. Investigations are conducted only when the following three elements exist:

- A threat or advocacy of force
- The apparent ability to carry out the proclaimed act
- The potential violation of a federal law

These guidelines give the FBI a consistent policy for initiating investigations. No one at the FBI can single out a group for surveillance without first making sure the situation meets the Attorney General's guidelines. Then, the AG must give the Bureau authorization to begin its investigation. The information uncovered is used to prevent terrorist activity and, whenever possible, to aid in the arrest and prosecution of persons or groups that have violated the law. Within the last five years, the FBI has conducted unprecedented investigations on foreign soil involving the bombing of the Cole Aircraft Carrier, U.S. embassies in Nigeria and Tanzania, and investigative presence in Afghanistan and Iraq. These investigations have involved both agent and administrative personnel with expertise in hostage negotiations, bombings, behavioral science, foresic evidence recovery, languages, major case management, and information technology.

The Atlanta Bomb Task Force—Domestic Terrorism

The FBI has discovered links among three different bombings in the Atlanta area: the Centennial Olympic Park bombing on July 27, 1996, the bombing at the Sandy Springs Professional Building on January 16, 1997, and the bombing at the Otherside Lounge on February 21, 1997. At the Olympic Park bombing during the Summer Olympics, one person was killed by the explosion and another suffered a fatal heart attack. The other two bombings were less spectacular, but intended to be more destructive. Each incident involved two separate explosions, with the second timed to target police and emergency personnel responding to the first.

THE "ARMY OF GOD" LETTER

THE BOMBING'S IN SANDY SPRINGS
AND MIDTOWN WERE CARRIED-OUT
BY UNITS OF THE ARMY OF GOD.
    THE ABORTION WAS THE TARGET
OF THE FIRST DEVICE. THE MURDER
IF 3.5 MILLION CHILDREN EVERY YEAR
WILL NOT BE "TOLERATED". THOSE
WHO PARTICIPATE IN ANYWAY IN
THE MURDER OF CHILDREN MAY
BE TARGETED FOR ATTACK. THE
ATTACK THEREFORE SERVES AS
A WARNING: ANYONE IN OR AROUND
FACILITIES THAT MURDER CHILDREN
MAY BECOME VICTIMS OF
RETRIBUTION. THE NEXT
    FACILITY TARGETED MAY NOT
BE EMPTY.
    THE SECOND DEVICE WAS
AIMED AT AGENT OF THE
SO-CALLED FEDERAL GOVERNMENT
I.E. A.T.F F.B.I. MARSHALL'S E.T.C.
WE DECLARE AND WILL WAGE
TOTAL WAR ON THE UNGODLY
COMMUNIST REGIME IN NEW YORK
AND YOUR LEGASLATIVE –
BUREAUCRATIC LACKEY'S IN
WASHINGTON. IT IS YOU WHO ARE
RESPOSIBLE AND PRESIDE OVER

Letter claiming responsibility for the Sandy Springs and Otherside bombings, from the Atlanta Bombing Case Consolidation, June 9, 1997 (continued on next page) (FBI Photo)

+HE MURDER OF CHILDREN AND
ISSUE THE POLICY OF UNGODLY
PREVERSION THATS DESTROYING OUR
~~THE~~ PEOPLE. WE WILL TARGET
ALL FACILITIES AND PERSONNell
OF THE FEDERAL GOVERNMENT.
THE ATTACK IN MIDTOWN WAS
AIMED AT THE SODOMITE BAR
(THE OTHERSIDE). WE WILL TARGET
SODOMITES, THERE ORGANIZATIONS,
AND ALL THOSE WHO PUSH THERE
AGENDA.
"DEATH TO THE NEW WORLD ORDER"

Foreign CounterIntelligence Program

One of the Bureau's most well-publicized counterespionage cases involved Aldrich Ames, a CIA agent who sold out to the KGB for almost $2 million. The Ames case has been well documented in several books; two of the best are *Confessions of a Spy: The Real Story of Aldrich Ames*, by Pete Earley, and *Killer Spy: The Inside Story of the FBI's Pursuit and Capture of Aldrich Ames, America's Deadliest Spy*, by Peter Maas.

The Mole

Aldrich Ames apparently never was the brightest bulb on the tree. His bosses gave him mediocre performance evaluations; he drank heavily, and was once found passed out in a gutter; he often napped at his desk after a multiple-martini lunch. Still, in September 1983, he was appointed the CIA's counterintelligence branch chief in Soviet operations. The job gave him access to a wealth of sensitive information, including the identities of Soviets working for the United States.

By early 1985, Rick Ames felt strapped for money. Two years earlier, while posted in Mexico City, he'd become involved with a woman working as a cultural attaché at the Colombian embassy. Rosario Casas Dupuy was an ambitious, forceful woman with a taste for the best—or at least the most expensive—of everything. Ames was in the middle of a divorce, and Rosario had come to live

with him in Arlington, Virginia. As a foreign
national in the United States on a tourist visa,
she couldn't work. She was bored and restless,
and complained constantly. Ames had piled up
tens of thousands of dollars in debt, and his
$45,000-a-year salary seemed pitifully
inadequate. Before he married Rosario, Rick felt
he needed a solid chunk of money—something to
settle his debts and get a fresh start. He
thought about a second job at a 7-11; he
considered bank robbery. Then he remembered his
most valuable asset, something worth a great
deal to certain people—information about U.S.
espionage.

On April 16, 1985, Ames set up a lunch
appointment with an employee at the Soviet
embassy, a man he was trying to recruit for the
CIA. Ames prepared a note addressed to the KGB
rezident posted at the Soviet embassy; he was
offering to sell the Soviets information about
the CIA's spying operations for $50,000 in cash.

Rick Ames got stood up for lunch. But,
fortified by several vodka martinis, he decided
to forge ahead anyway. He drove straight to the
Soviet embassy and handed the security guard an
envelope addressed to the KGB rezident, using
the man's KGB code name. Within a month, Ames had
his $50,000, and a new career as a spy. He

excelled in his career as a mole in a way he
never had while working "above ground."

Over the next five years, Rick Ames sold
tremendous amounts of information to the
Soviets. He betrayed as many as 20 agents
working for the United States; several of these
men were promptly executed, leaving their
families in the Soviet Union destitute and
disgraced. In exchange, Ames received enough
money to support himself and Rosario in the
manner she wanted to become accustomed to:
expensive vacations, live-in servants, designer
dresses, custom-tailored silk suits, Rolex and
Gucci watches, a Jaguar sports car, cosmetic
caps for his unattractive teeth, $5,000-a-month
phone bills for chatty calls to her mother in
Colombia. When they bought a half-million dollar
house in the DC suburbs, they paid cash.

This conspicuous consumption didn't go
unnoticed; when anyone asked, Ames said Rosario
had inherited the money. He told Rosario herself
that a friend, "Robert from Chicago," had given
him money to invest; Ames had done well, and the
free-flowing cash was his percentage of the
profits. Rosario never questioned this
explanation—why Robert never called, visited,
or wrote; why anyone would give Ames so much
money to invest; how he managed to do so well
after botching his own finances so thoroughly.

While the Ameses spent their blood money, the CIA was trying to discover what had gone wrong. Most of the executions took place in 1985, and the KGB managed to direct suspicion to a disgruntled former employee who'd threatened to expose the Agency's secrets. When the losses seemed to subside, so did the CIA's eagerness to find the mole some suspected was operating in their midst.

But some CIA employees never let the issue drop. In 1988, when the CIA formed a Counterintelligence Center at Langley, one of the investigators assigned to the new unit was Dan Payne. Earlier investigations of the 1985 murders had tried to match the leaked information with those who had access to it. Payne was eager to try a different approach, looking for CIA employees who seemed to be living beyond their means.

Ames's name soon surfaced, but hard proof was lacking. The CIA's Office of Security passed Ames on his regularly scheduled security clearance, despite signs of deception on the polygraph. Payne and his boss, Jeanne Vertefeuille, had to move on to other cases.

Finally, in early 1991, Vertefeuille asked her new boss if she could devote herself full time to the 1985 losses. She was close to retirement, and she really wanted to focus on

this project, to try to get some answers before
she left the Agency.

At this point, the FBI got involved. In 1985,
the Bureau had investigated why two of its
Soviet spies had been arrested and executed; by
1987 the investigators concluded they just
didn't have enough information to come to a
conclusion. But the FBI still wanted answers.

The new dual-agency, mole-hunt task force
consisted of Jeanne Vertefueille and CIA
investigator Sandy Grimes, plus James P.
Milburn, one of the FBI's Soviet experts, and
Jim Holt, a veteran FBI agent.

For the first time in this investigation or
any other, there was complete cooperation
between the two agencies. Vertefueille gave the
FBI agents unrestricted access to all the CIA's
records, except for medical and psychological
files.

Gradually, methodically, the task force
narrowed its focus to Ames. Dan Payne was asked
to investigate Ames's finances; he was shocked
to discover that a man whose salary was barely
$70,000 a year was spending $200,000 a year on
credit card charges alone. Sandy Grimes co-
nstructed a meticulous timeline of events in
Rick Ames's life and career; she noticed an
interesting pattern. Within a day or two after a
visit with a Soviet contact, Ames would deposit

several thousand dollars in his checking or savings accounts. These deposits were always just under $10,000—the legal cutoff for federal reporting.

By the end of 1992, Dan Payne had discovered several Swiss bank accounts Ames maintained. Payne calculated that in the past six years, Ames had received $1.3 million from unknown sources. The task force was convinced they'd found their mole.

Once Ames was identified as the chief suspect, the FBI's Washington Field Office organized an investigation, with Special Agent Les Wiser at its head. The full-scale investigation, with round-the-clock surveillance and wiretaps, began in May 1993. FBI agents even "borrowed" Ames's household garbage in the middle of the night, carting it away and sorting through it before returning it to the curb. Agents even took careful notes of the placement of the top layer of trash, so they could duplicate it before bringing back to the Ames home. Everything the agents discovered through the surveillance confirmed their suspicions, but they weren't able to gather enough hard evidence to move forward.

The investigation continued at this plateau for almost four months, and the risk that Ames would realize he was being scrutinized increased every day. Then there was one terrible day in early September 1993, when a series of miscommunications and equipment failures let Ames escape surveillance and make a dead drop.

Wiser and his agents were desperate for a breakthrough. Against explicit orders from Wiser's boss, they made one more trash pickup, on the night of September 15. This time, they hit pay dirt. Buried among the cereal boxes and used paper towels and other household garbage, the Agents found a yellow sticky note torn into bits. When they reassembled the pieces, the note, in Ames's handwriting, read: "I am ready to meet at B on 1 Oct." The agents knew this meant Ames was planning a meeting with his handlers in Bogota, Colombia. Finally, they had hard evidence of Ames's activities. According to Maas, Wiser's boss called his decision to defy direct orders to terminate the trash pickups "a marvelous piece of insubordination."

The October 1 meeting between Ames and his handlers was canceled, but other breakthroughs followed. Wiretaps revealed that Rick and Rosario were planning to attend a wedding out of town in late October; the FBI obtained a search warrant and searched the house while they were away. They found a KBG officer's home phone number scribbled down in Rick's handwriting, and a note rescheduling the Bogota meeting for

November 1. On Ames's computer, agents found several letters to his handler, detailing meeting times and places and information that would be passed.

The FBI now had more than enough evidence to demonstrate that Rick was a mole. However, the investigation continued; the Department of Justice wanted to catch Rick in the act.

The FBI staked out Ames at the meeting place in Bogota. However, he again evaded surveillance. There were no contacts between Rick and his handlers for the rest of 1993. However, wiretaps did record conversations between Rick and Rosario that made it clear that she was aware of his spying activities; this evidence would become crucial during the prosecution.

Finally, on February 21, 1994, the move was made to arrest both Ames and his wife. FBI Agents swooped down on Ames's Jaguar as he drove through his neighborhood on that quiet Presidents' Day morning. As he was pushed into a waiting car, Ames muttered to himself, "Think, think, think."

But it was too late for that. Ames was charged with espionage. Rosario Ames was arrested at their home and charged with assisting him.

FBI Agent Julie Johnson had listened to hours and hours of wiretapped conversations between Rick and Rosario; she had real insight into their relationship and their personalities. She advised the agents interviewing Rosario to treat her with respect; try to bully her, and she'll blow up, Johnson warned. But Johnson felt that given a chance, Rosario would turn over on Rick.

Johnson was right. Once the agents interviewing Rosario pointed out her lies and contradictions, she told them she was tired of playing games. "Rick works for the Russians," she said.

The evidence against Ames was devastating—including a letter from his KGB handler listing what Ames had been paid and what was being held for him. The cash total came to $2.7 million; that doesn't count the value of a riverfront dacha set aside for the day when the KGB's valued spy might wish to retire to Russia. Despite the case against him, Ames's attorney, Plato Cacheris, advised him to fight. Cacheris argued that there was only one way to get a deal for himself and for Rosario—Ames had to play hardball, instead of revealing his weakness, his concern for Rosario.

But Ames insisted on cooperating. He didn't want Rosario to go through a trial. At first,

Rosario wanted to push forward, protesting her innocence in court. Then the prosecutor invited Rosario and her lawyer to listen to wiretap evidence he planned to play in court. As Earley describes them, the tapes capture Rosario "sniveling about money, griping at [their young son] Paul, belittling her friends, and constantly degrading and chiding Rick. She sounded arrogant, contemptuous, totally self-absorbed and, worst of all, greedy." It was also clear from the tapes that she was fully aware of Rick's dealings with the Soviets; while he was in Bogota, she harangued him about putting the documents and cash in his carry-on luggage, rather than entrusting them to airline baggage handlers.

In the end, both Rick and Rosario opted for a plea bargain. Rick received life in prison without possibility of parole; Rosario's sentencing was delayed until Rick was fully debriefed. Rick did cooperate, and Rosario was sentenced to a five-year term. Custody of Paul, their son, was awarded to Rosario's mother while Rosario serves out her sentence. Unprecedented cooperation between the CIA and FBI was vital to this outcome of this case.

The New Espionage

Of course, there's no longer a KGB or a Soviet Union to recruit spies. But the end of the "evil empire" hasn't brought about the end of espionage. Instead, it has brought new threats from new sources—the old Soviet republics, the emerging Asian powers. The threat of espionage hasn't decreased; in fact, in some areas it has grown and become more difficult to assess and predict. And it remains a major problem. According to some estimates, espionage currently costs the United States economy $100 billion per year.

You won't ever hear much in the media about the FBI's ongoing foreign counterintelligence work. Unlike criminal investigations, espionage and espionage-related matters usually don't lead to arrest and prosecution. Instead, the goal is to neutralize the threat; the public never becomes aware of most of the program's activities.

Those activities cover spying on government and private industry. Because of our country's technological and business strength, companies and research institutions as well as government entities continue to be prime targets of foreign intelligence services. The FBI investigates wherever and whenever a foreign organization conducts clandestine intelligence activities in the United States.

In fact, there's so much spying directed at business interests that the FBI puts a special focus on economic espionage. The Bureau defines economic espionage as follows:

"Foreign power-sponsored or coordinated intelligence activity directed at the U.S. government or U.S. corporations, establishments, or persons designed to unlawfully and clandestinely obtain sensitive financial, trade, or economic policy information; proprietary economic information; critical technologies; or to unlawfully or clandestinely influence sensitive economic policy decisions."

The opportunities for economic espionage, and the value of the information the spies are after, will just continue to grow. As multinational companies expand their operations, and as technology connects individuals and organizations around the globe, information becomes more valuable and harder to protect. And information doesn't have to be "classified" to be valuable. Patents, technical plans, drafts of public policy documents—anything that deals with sensitive economic, technological, or governmental matters, on any level, can catch a spy's eye.

Think about Microsoft, or Java, or any other software company. A significant percentage of the company's budget consists of R&D—research and development into better, more efficient computer applications. If a foreign company can get its hands on the end product, leapfrogging over the expensive R&D process, they'll be that much ahead.

And software is just one example; the United States leads the world in intellectual property development—software, technological innovations, manufacturing improvements, all sorts of ideas and discoveries with economic value. The theft or misappropriation of this intellectual property can save foreign companies and governments billions of dollars; saving all that money allows those companies and governments to sell their products at a lower cost, increasing their market share and profit margins. In a global market, that costs the United States economy even more money.

You can't spot a spy by his trench coat and shifty eyes. Recent surveys show that corporate insiders account for up to 75 percent of U.S. technology loss. Often, these spies are American citizens acting on their own to sell information to foreign intelligence services.

You can be part of that human factor. Raise your security awareness. Report any suspected espionage activity to the FBI. This doesn't mean you should play spy-counterspy with the guy in the cubicle down the way. But look out for the following:

- Unauthorized attempts to view records or plans
- Scavenging through trash
- Eavesdropping on live or telephone conversations

163

- Questions from persons who have no need to know certain information to do their job
- Persons found outside their normal work areas or at unusual hours

A recent study by the American Society for Industrial Security has put the cost of the theft of trade secrets from U.S. business at $2 billion per month. The Economic Espionage Act of 1996 was signed into law by President Bill Clinton on October 11, 1996. This created federal criminal jurisdiction regarding both state-sponsored and commercial theft of trade secrets. Misappropriation or theft of both intangible and tangible property is a crime under the Act. The FBI is currently involved in investigations in both state-sponsored and commercial theft of trade secrets.

Operation Counter Copy

The FBI's efforts regarding the investigation of Intellectual Property Right (IPR) criminal investigations centers on locating and identifying the producers, principal distributors, and publishers of unauthorized trademarks and/or copyrighted products in order to eliminate the sources of illicit productions. These cases typically involve major manufacturers of illegally produced goods that lead to either significant financial losses to victim companies or potential risks to the health and welfare of the general public.

The FBI investigates the illegal manufacturing and distribution trademarked items and copyrightable work. This covers, among other things, motion pictures, sound recordings (tapes and records), audiovisual works (video games), computer software, musical compositions (sheet music), television shows, books, and art objects. The FBI is also seeing more investigations regarding thefts of trade secrets.

The FBI's investigative experience has shown that the most effective way to identify manufacturers and distributors is to buy copies of suspicious items and confirm that the items are unauthorized duplications. Using the counterfeits as evidence, investigators can then request a search warrant to seize the contraband and related duplication equipment. Prosecution of retailers usually depends on two things: their awareness of the illegal counterfeiting, and the extent of their cooperation with the investigation and prosecution of major suppliers.

In April 1996, the U.S. Trade Representative confronted Chinese representatives about China's widespread piracy of American movies, records, and computer software. FBI Director Freeh later met with the Acting U.S. Trade Representative and discussed the global problem of IPR infringement. In a followup measure, the FBI initiated Operation Counter Copy to further identify and address the growing IPR infringement problem.

Operation Counter Copy has brought together IPR investigations from eleven FBI offices across the country. The cases involve copyright infringement of motion pictures, sound recordings, and computer software, as well as trademark infringement matters. The FBI works closely with the various related industries including the Motion Picture Association, Business Software Alliance, and the Recording Industry Association of America in order to better address this crime problem. This is an ongoing initiative that will be expanding internationally through cooperation with foreign law enforcement authorities.

Organized Crime and Drug Program

The FBI's organized crime program as resulted in numerous high profile cases. Organized crime has developed beyond the stereotypical Italian/Sicilian family structure. The FBI is now involved in criminal organizations from Russia, Colombia, Mexico, Asia, and even domestic gangs. Here are are federal violations often associated with organized crime :

- Drug matters
- Racketeer Influenced and Corrupt Organizations (RICO) matters

- Criminal enterprise investigations
- Labor racketeering
- Money laundering
- Organized crime/Drug Enforcement Task Force matters

The FBI has an arsenal of weapons at its disposal: asset forfeiture laws, sophisticated investigative techniques, and a nationwide and international law enforcement network. The most significant tool used in fighting organized crime passed in 1970: the Racketeer Influenced and Corrupt Organizations (RICO) statute. Under the criminal and civil RICO provisions, FBI Special Agents and other law enforcement officials are authorized to use undercover operations, court-ordered electronic surveillance (such as wiretaps), informants and cooperating witnesses, and consensual monitoring (or "wearing a wire").

I just mentioned a couple of fairly controversial issues: use of wiretapping and use of informants.

First, contrary to what you may have seen in the movies, wiretapping is not used that often, and it's used only in fighting serious crimes such as major drug dealing, terrorism and, as you saw in the Ames case, espionage. No FBI Special Agent—or anyone else in the Bureau—can install a wiretap on his own. Before a wiretap can be put in place, the FBI has to show probable cause that the wiretap is likely to provide evidence of a felony violation of federal law. A federal judge—someone who has no stake in the outcome—evaluates the agent's evidence; based on that evidence, the judge either authorizes the wiretap, or tells the agent to come back with a more convincing legal argument. While the wiretap is operating, the judge monitors how it's used, and he or she can shut it down at any time if it's being abused. Anyone—including a Special Agent—who installs a wiretap without following these rules commits a serious felony.

Second, I feel that the use of informants has gotten a bad rap in the media. Informants are "rats" and "snitches," while the people who don't give up any information are "stand-up guys." People become informants for all kinds of reasons—they want money, they're looking for revenge, they've got a troubled conscience. Of course some informants are sleazy. Most law-abiding, clean-living citizens don't hang out with chronic law breakers. The fact is, when you're trying to gather intelligence about law-breaking groups, closed societies that isolate themselves from the larger culture, you're going to need informants to get the job done.

U.S. courts recognize the use of informants as lawful, even essential. But the courts also realize that use of informants can involve serious issues: deception, privacy violations, involvement with people who have questionable motives or reliability. To handle these issues, the Attorney General developed specific guidelines regulating the FBI's use of informants. Agents carefully supervise the informants' activities and evaluate their information to make sure nothing about the investigation violates the legal rights of individuals under investigation.

Informants don't become FBI employees, even if they're paid by the FBI. They're not hired or trained by the FBI, and the FBI won't necessarily intervene in any criminal cases pending against the informant.

Drug trafficking is closely allied with organized crime, which is why the two areas are combined in one program. After years of working against an ever-changing drug trade, in 1980 the FBI developed the Enterprise Theory of Investigation from the work of lawyer and scholar Robert Bakke, which focuses investigations and prosecutions on entire criminal enterprises rather than on individuals.

One of the most successful operations in FBI history unfolded over years and years of frustrating work, and relied on both those controversial investigation methods—wiretaps and informants.

The Teflon Don

For decades, New York City was the epicenter of organized crime activity. Five families had a stranglehold on several vital industries: construction, garbage disposal, and garment manufacturing, among others. They also controlled shipping through New York's airports and docks. The mob set their own prices for their services; anyone who tried undercut them, or interfere with their business in any way, faced threats and intimidation, beatings, destruction of their property, even murder. Organized crime may look glamorous and exciting in the movies, but it's pretty ugly in real life; plenty of people lost their livelihood, and their lives, trying to go up against the mob.

By 1980, the FBI's New York Field Office had organized five squads focusing on the five major organized crime families. This was intensive, dedicated work. Agents who have dedicated a major portion of their careers to organized crime find out all about the "family," memorizing names and relationships. It's not something you can just pick up in a year or two and call yourself an expert. These guys can name birthdays, anniversaries, all the relationships—it's like they're a part of the family."

The most powerful of New York's five families was the Gambino family, led for years by Paul Castellano. On December 16, 1985, Castellano was murdered, shot to death in front of a Manhattan steak house. A relatively minor mobster named John Gotti took over the Gambinos, and ushered in a new era of organized crime.

Earlier bosses kept a low profile, but Gotti seemed to thrive on attention. He got the nickname "Dapper Don" in honor of his expensive tailored suits, expensive Italian shoes, and expensive, blow-dried coiffure—not exactly a look favored by most plumbers, which was Gotti's declared profession. He appeared on the cover of TIME magazine. He hosted lavish, and blatantly illegal, Fourth of July fireworks displays in his Queens neighborhood.

Over the years, FBI wiretap recordings had helped convict the heads of four Mafia families, but Gotti was more cautious. Agents installed bugs in Gotti's headquarters, the Ravenite Social Club in Manhattan's Little Italy. Even though 20 or 30 associates visited the Ravenite almost every day, Gotti never discussed any sensitive issues within range of the listening devices. In December 1988, the squad pulled back to review their operations.

The agents scrutinized videotapes, watching everyone who entered and exited the Ravenite. They reread all the surveillance reports. They listened again and again to the audiotapes they'd recorded. They pumped their informants for information. Finally, they realized that Gotti seemed to be holding his most sensitive conversations in four places: a hallway at the back of the club, a vacant second-floor apartment above it, the sidewalk just outside, and an office a mile or so away, in Manhattan's garment district.

The squad got authorization to plant new bugs in those locations, and within a week the FBI had the information they needed. In an interview with New York Newsday, J. Bruce Mouw, head of the FBI's Gambino squad, described the haul: "They were getting dynamite conversations. Now, we were on the right track. Gotti felt totally secure. He thought he had fooled everyone, so he wasn't as careful as with his conversation."

While the investigations were continuing, Gotti was earning another nickname—"The Teflon Don." In 1986, the New York District Attorney brought an assault case against Gotti, but the case was dismissed when the plaintiff refused to press charges. In 1987, Gotti was acquitted of federal racketeering charges; five years later, a juror in that trial would be convicted of accepting $60,000 in exchange for his vote for acquittal. In 1990, Gotti was acquitted on state assault charges. Finally, in 1992, armed with the

"dynamite" audiotapes and the testimony of a mob
turncoat, Sammy Gravano, the prosecutors won.
Gotti was convicted of thirteen counts of murder
and racketeering. He was sentenced to life in
prison without possibility of parole.

Violent Crimes and Major Offenders Program

This is the FBI's broadest investigative program, and probably its most visible. It covers the following crimes, among others:

- Kidnapping and extortion
- Sexual exploitation of children
- Tampering with consumer products
- Fugitives wanted as a result of FBI investigations
- Escaped federal prisoners (some instances)
- Probation/parole violations (some instances)
- Unlawful flight to avoid prosecution (including parental-kidnapping fugitives)
- Crime on Indian reservations
- Theft of government property
- Interstate transportation of stolen motor vehicles
- Interstate transportation of stolen property
- Theft from interstate shipments
- Assaulting, kidnapping or killing the president, vice president, or a member of congress
- Bank robbery, burglary, or larceny
- Crime aboard aircraft

The case I'm going to tell you about illustrates several aspects of investigating violent crimes: the devastation encountered; the confusing, contradictory evidence; how the preconceptions of a primary investigator can affect the accuracy of a profile; how the determination of one law enforcement officer can ensure that justice does prevail.

The Wrong Guy

When I came across this case, it was a murder. One horrible murder.

In late January 1984, two police detectives from Arlington, Virginia—Robert Carrig and Chuck Shelton—asked for a profile on the perpetrator in Carolyn Hamm's murder. Sometime on January 23, Hamm had been raped and killed. The killer entered her home through a basement window and surprised her when she returned home. Police found a knife the perpetrator used to control her. He'd then stripped her, bound her with cords found in the house, raped her, and strangled her to death. Carrig and Shelton brought us crime scene photos and autopsy reports to work with—no other case linkages, little forensic evidence.

Roy Hazelwood and I talked to the detectives; Roy came up with a profile I agreed with. There were elements of both organized and disorganized behavior at the crime scene; this could point to two killers, or to one killer with two divergent aspects to his personality. Because Hamm was white, we predicted that the killer was white. This kind of crime rarely crossed racial boundaries.

Meanwhile, Arlington Detective Joe Horgas was looking at the case, too. Horgas had been up for the next murder investigation in the department rotation, but when Hamm was murdered, he was away on vacation. The case went to Carrig and Shelton.

Still, Horgas felt a connection to the case; he decided to just take a look at reports of break-ins and sexual assaults near the time of the murder. He discovered two break-ins reported within days of Hamm's murder, within blocks of her home. Elements of both crimes seemed to reflect elements in the killing, and they also seemed to be related to a series of rapes in the Arlington area—nine reported rapes since 1983. Witnesses described the perpetrator as a black male, about five-ten, slight, wearing a mask.

When Horgas approached his supervisor with his theory that the break-ins, the rapes, and Hamm's murder were all linked, his supervisor reminded him that the murder case wasn't his— but he gave Horgas the okay to continue investigating the break-in connection. Horgas sent out a teletype to police departments in the area, describing the "black masked rapist" and hoping someone had spotted him.

On February 6, 1984, Arlington police arrested David Vasquez for Hamm's murder. Vasquez had recently moved out of the area, but witnesses reported seeing him near Hamm's home around the time of the murder. When they searched the room where Vasquez had lived, investigators found Penthouse-type magazines, along with peeping-Tom photographs of various women in their homes. One of the magazines contained a photograph showing a woman tied up in a way similar to the way Hamm had been bound.

After an interrogation that took place over several days, Vasquez confessed to Carolyn Hamm's murder.

There were problems with the case. Hair samples from the scene were similar to Vasquez's pubic hair, but semen samples couldn't be matched to him. Vasquez didn't drive, and at the time of Hamm's murder, he lived at least an hour away. He was smaller than Hamm and would have had trouble controlling her physically; he wasn't nearly as intelligent as Hamm and couldn't have dominated her mentally.

Based partly on our profile, Arlington police figured that Vasquez had been the less mature, less organized, of two perpetrators. They pushed Vasquez to name his accomplice, but Vasquez insisted there was no accomplice. He accepted a plea bargain and was sentenced to 35 years in prison. Hamm's murder was solved.

Almost four years later, on December 1, 1987, the body of Susan Tucker was discovered in her bedroom, nude and bound. Detective Joe Horgas was assigned to the case.

Looking at the scene, Horgas immediately thought of Carolyn Hamm's murder. There were similarities in the method of entry, the binding, the killing itself, the victimology. The women's homes were only blocks apart.

Horgas drove to Buckingham Correction Center to interview David Vasquez. The interview was disturbing, in ways Horgas never expected.

Vasquez desperately wanted out. He cried while talking to Horgas; he'd been assaulted over and over in the prison, and Horgas was his very first visitor. But as miserable as Vasquez was, he didn't give up the name of his accomplice. He couldn't give Horgas any useful information at all.

Horgas left the prison worried about two terrible possibilities. One, Vasquez had been locked up for a crime he didn't commit. Two, the real perpetrator was still out there, still killing.

When Horgas took a look at the Hamm investigation, he became even more convinced that Vasquez was the wrong guy. Vasquez had been interrogated in a way that was sure to confuse and overwhelm his limited mental abilities; his confession hadn't contained any information the investigators didn't already know. To Horgas, the indicators of a second partner now seemed to point to another perpetrator altogether.

Horgas went back to his original theory: a link between the rapes committed by the "black masked rapist," the break-ins, Hamm's murder, and now Tucker's murder. He found a couple of promising leads, but the real breakthrough came when Horgas came across a teletype from the Richmond, Virginia PD, describing a murder strikingly similar to Tucker's. This killing had taken place on October 6, 1987, just two months before.

When Horgas called the Richmond cops, he found out there were even more similarities than described in the teletype—and another rape-murder, possibly related, had happened since. The Richmond cops were dubious about Horgas's theory, but they invited him to a task force meeting anyway.

That openness, and Horgas's determination, would be the keys to solving the case.

Richmond detectives Glen Williams and Ray Williams were in charge of the Tucker investigation. (They aren't related, but everyone in the department calls them "the Williams boys.") They were under a tremendous amount of pressure. Murders are relatively uncommon in Richmond, and a serial rapist-murderer was almost unheard of. Richmond residents were panicking, and there was a lot of media scrutiny. The department poured resources into the investigation.

The Williams boys asked for help from the FBI's profiling unit; Jud Ray and Tom Salp drove down to meet with them. The police presented information on their two murders and, based on that presentation, Jud and Tom came up with a profile.

Those of you who read Mindhunter may remember Jud Ray. For those of you who aren't familiar with him, let me just put in a word here. Jud's a fine agent, and an excellent profiler. He also brings a couple of unusual viewpoints to his work. Unlike most members of the profiling unit—at least when I was there—Jud is a black man from the rural South. He's also the survivor of a murder attempt; his wife very nearly succeeded in having him shot to death. That experience, among other things, gives him real empathy for victims, and an uncanny ability to "read" a scene from the victim's point of view.

Jud and Tom pointed out that the killer was somewhat sophisticated, leaving no prints or obvious clues; this indicated he had some experience with the criminal system and had learned from the experience—which meant the perpetrator was reasonably intelligent. The killings took place on Friday nights; he probably had a full-time job. The binding and control of the victims required real physical strength. Petecchial hemorrhages and other evidence indicated that in each case, the killer had strangled the woman, released the ligature, strangled her again, released her again—over and over, until the woman finally died. This was a clear indication of sexual sadism, and the behavior seemed to be escalating. Other factors indicated a loner, someone probably not in a relationship with a woman and not likely to brag about his crimes. Statistically speaking, the killer was probably a white man.

In November 1987, the killer struck again. His victim, Diane Cho, was much younger than the previous targets, but there were unmistakable similarities. Tests on semen at the scenes linked the Cho, Davis, and Hellams murders.

Meanwhile, Joe Horgas was pursuing his theory. He was convinced that the Hamm and Tucker murders in Arlington and the three murders in Richmond were all committed by a "black masked rapist" reported in both areas. Preliminary serological testing linked the Tucker killer to the Richmond murders. Horgas formed a task force to investigate the Tucker murder and started reinvestigating the Arlington rapes.

He called the Investigative Support Unit and asked for a meeting; on December 29, Steve Mardigian and Jud Ray drove down to Arlington. Horgas's presentation was comprehensive, organized, and thorough. And he finally got some support for his theory.

Steve and Jud agreed that there was good reason to think that the Arlington and Richmond murders were linked, and that all the murders were linked to the "black masked rapist" crimes. There were just too many similarities. Jud and Steve felt that the rapes were rehearsals for the murders; the killer perfected his technique before escalating his crimes.

Finally, Horgas revealed that the Hamm case was closed—a killer had been apprehended and sentenced. He described Vasquez and asked whether the agents thought he could have been the more submissive of two criminal partners.

This put everything in a new light. Jud and Steve stressed that they'd need to do a more intensive review of the case materials to give a more definitive answer, but based on what they'd seen, the answer was no. These crimes seemed to be the work of someone who acted alone, someone who wouldn't want or need a partner.

Finally, the three investigators talked about the issue of the perpetrator's race. Why had the earlier profiles predicted a white man?

Well, statistically, it was the right answer.
The vast majority of serial killers are white
men. Black men rarely commit these kinds of
crimes, and when they do, as in the case of Wayne
Williams, the Atlanta child murderer, their
victims are almost always black, too. This may
be changing, and Jud has some interesting
theories about why that is.

Jud's thinking is based on his experience as a
cop and as a profiler, but also as a black man
raised in the rural South. "There is a noticeable
difference in the psychopathology of black sexual
offenders and white sexual offenders regarding the
way they each treat the living or dead body," Jud
says. Black offenders rarely insert foreign
objects, sexually mutilate the body, or commit
other kinds of depravity common among white
offenders. Jud thinks this will hold true for
blacks who remain outside the American mainstream.
But as minorities become more integrated into the
culture, their criminal signatures will also begin
to reflect those of the larger culture.

For instance, George Russell Jr. was an
intelligent, middle-class black man who raped
and killed several Seattle-area women in 1990.
Like the classic white sexual predator, Russell
arranged his victims in degrading poses. One
woman was left with a rifle shoved into her
vagina. Russell was fully integrated into the

mainstream culture; he moved easily in predominantly white circles. This seems to confirm Jud's theory that culture, rather than race itself, is the significant factor in determining a killer's signature.

The important point to remember is that profiles are predictions, not descriptions. Investigators shouldn't rely on a profile to the exclusion of other evidence. Horgas saw the similarities in the way the rapes and the murders were carried out; those similarities outweighed the contradiction between the profile prediction and the witness descriptions of a black man. Horgas's instincts were sound.

Jud, Steve and Horgas came up with an investigative strategy. Horgas focused on the rapes, since those cases were open and the victims were still alive and could be interviewed. Because the rapes had stopped about the time of Vasquez's arrest, then resumed in Richmond almost four years later, the perpetrator had probably been sent to jail for a relatively minor offense, such as burglary.

Horgas started sifting through arrest and parole records, but the task was overwhelming. He took a break and searched his own memory for clues. Several years before, he'd worked the section of the city where the first rapes had occurred; maybe he'd run into the rapist then.

He had. Horgas remembered a young man named
Timothy Spencer—suspected of burglary, accused
of setting fire to his mother's home. One of the
rape victims had been locked in the trunk of her
car, which was then set on fire.

Horgas called up Spencer's records and found
that he'd been convicted of burglary on January
29, 1984, and released to a halfway house in
Richmond on September 4, 1987. Details of the
burglary matched up with details of the murders.

Horgas conferred with Richmond police, who
set up surveillance on Spencer. But after a
week, when they saw nothing suspicious, they
discontinued the surveillance. On January 20,
1988, Horgas obtained an arrest warrant for
Spencer and brought him in.

Though Spencer never confessed, DNA and
other forensic evidence clinched the case
against him. On July 16, 1988, he was found
guilty of Susan Tucker's murder; three other
murder convictions followed, for the killings of
Debbie Davis, Susan Hellams, and Diane Cho in
Richmond. He was executed on April 27, 1994.

But what about David Vasquez? Steve
Mardigian created a detailed chart that sorted
out all the information known about the Hamm
case, as well as the rapes, burglaries, and the
other murders. He brought the chart to me and
each of us analyzed it independently before we

conferred. We came to the same conclusion: There
was no way two people had committed these
crimes. There was no way David Vasquez committed
them, either. He didn't have the mental or
physical capacity to handle them; nothing in his
history or current behavior indicated he was a
sexual sadist, as the killer definitely was.

On October 18, 1988, we sent a five-page
report to the Arlington County Commonwealth
Attorney, presenting our conclusion that the man
who'd murdered Tucker, Hellams, and Cho had also
murdered Carolyn Hamm. We supported the request
from Joe Horgas and the Arlington Police
Department that David Vasquez receive a pardon
from the governor.

David Vasquez was finally released from
prison on January 4, 1989. He might still be
there, if Joe Horgas hadn't been so astute and so
determined to see real justice done.

White-Collar Crime Program

A reporter once asked Willie Sutton, a bank robber in the 1940s, why he
robbed banks. His reply: "That's where the money is." That little story illustrates a basic fact about white-collar criminals: They go where the money is.

Of course there's still a lot of money in banks, but today there's even more
money in places Willie Sutton never dreamed about. Board rooms and the
company pension funds seem to be the new vaults raided by those in the
executive suites. Martha Stewart, Inc., the United Nations, and prominent

healthcare companies are the landscape of high profile white collar crime. "Follow the money" is an exhortation in white collar investigations. Stock manipulation, corruption of public officials, telemarketing, and cyber-crimes all fall into the category of white collar work.

The FBI directs a large-scale investigative operation known as Innocent Images designed to track the exploitation of children over the internet; specifically the sale and purchase of child pornography. These investigations are conducted by using interagency task forces where both police and FBI agents often enter chat rooms and position themselves as children vulnerable to the suggestions of predators. Numerous arrests and child porn rings have been dismantled due to these efforts.

The FBI's impact in the area of Healthcare fraud has also been tremendous. Major cases against prominent physicians, nursing homes, hospitals, and billing networks have been successfully prosecuted. Medicare fraud is an exceptionally complex matter and impacts patient welfare, resources for legitimate services, and large sums of money. These cases are directed by FBI task forces, and can often involve acts of violence such as killing witnesses, domestic terrorism, and bodily threats against case agents. Many violators, even some organized crime figures, are currently involved in healthcare fraud because it is so lucrative. White-collar crimes run the gamut—small-time to multimillion-dollar. Early in his career, Doug Rhoads had to figure out how to handle a whole series of relatively small swindles:

"Shortly after I got to Lubbock, there was a huge tornado. Flattened half the town, killed I don't know how many people. After anything like that, you get federal agencies coming in to help. So the Small Business Administration gets set up to loan money to the mom-and-pop type businesses that were wiped out. About half the people looking for money were legitimate and needed the money, and half of them were frauds. For instance, a guy said he had a dry-cleaning business with millions of dollars in equipment and clothing in there, when he had a tenth of that. Another guy has a used car lot, he says he had 20 cars destroyed when he had three.

"All of a sudden, I've got about 20 of these SBA fraud cases to deal with. Had no clue where to start, no idea what the SBA statute even said. So I got hold of the assistant U.S. attorney, and we looked up the statute. Then I just started interviewing people. If I had a question, I'd get with a veteran agent. It isn't brain surgery, it's just work. Talking to people. That's 90 percent of what the bureau does. That's how you learn, get a bunch of cases and just start doing them."

While all FBI offices handle isolated instances of white-collar crime, the Bureau also investigates large-scale fraud by organized groups. The FBI also concentrates on mortgage loan fraud, an investigation aimed at loan brokers, appraisers, accountants, and attorneys engaged in conspiracies to defraud lending institutions.

The FBI also pursues illegal telemarketing aggressively; the Senior Sentinel project is an outstanding example of proactive and effective investigation.

Senior Sentinel

Unscrupulous telemarketers often target senior citizens, preying on those who seem vulnerable to their fast-talking schemes. In 1993, the San Diego Division of the FBI responded to complaints of telemarketing fraud aimed at seniors by training potential victims to help combat the problem.

Senior Sentinel used citizen volunteers, many referred to the Bureau by the American Association of Retired Persons (AARP). These volunteers had a special monitored phone line installed in their homes, with installation and maintenance costs covered by the FBI. The volunteers were trained in how to respond to telemarketers' pitches, which were recorded. In response to a fraudulent-sounding pitch, the volunteers provided money orders or "sight drafts" (a kind of electronic transfer). Once the volunteer sent in money, his or her name and phone number were "reloaded" and sold to other telemarketers. Soon, the volunteer would be fielding a stream of calls from other shady telemarketers—and the cycle would begin again.

This innovative program resulted in exceptionally strong prosecutions. The recording became direct evidence be used in court; the "prize"—usually a cheap gadget worth a lot less than promised—was additional evidence. I'm sure it made a real impression on the juries, hearing the lavish description of the prize and then seeing the shoddy reality.

Senior Sentinel was so successful that the FBI rolled it out nationwide in 1995. It's currently operated as a joint effort of the FBI, the U.S. Attorney's Office, the Internal Revenue Service, the Federal Trade Commission, and local, state and federal law enforcement.

The FBI "franchised" the citizen volunteer technique, which has been adopted by 38 Field Offices across the country. In each region, copies of the tape recordings are forwarded to a central location, where they're organized according to type of scheme, the company's name and location, and the phone name of the individual solicitor. Thousands of fraudulent pitches have been recorded as a result of Senior Sentinel; the tapes are available to any law enforcement agencies conducting telemarketing investigations.

Over the last several years, Senior Sentinel has provided the FBI and other law enforcement agencies with vast amounts of information about the structure and functioning of illegal telemarketing operations. This intelligence continues to be invaluable in combating this crime problem.

SUCCESS IN ALL AREAS

So you see, the immensely diversified investigative capability of the FBI absolutely depends on the diversity of its personnel. The FBI has historically recruited accountants and lawyers, but the Bureau knows clearly it must recruit personnel from all walks of life and career to address the vastness of its mission. Success in the assignments detailed in this chapter requires individuals of differing temperment, background and personal experience, education, practical work experience, and specialized military or scientific ability. Importantly, it requires you have no hesitation relating and speaking with persons of various backgrounds and circumstances. The Bureau knows the way someone looks on paper is not the whole story. I like to think the FBI has a massive environment in which to self-actualize and translate your specific skills into an enormous service to your country.

CHAPTER

The FBI Mission
Post-September 11

5

The FBI's mission and direction has changed dramatically since the September 11, 2001 attacks on the World Trade Center and the Pentagon, adjusting priorities 360 degrees. Protection of United States from terrorist attacks has replaced drugs and violent crime as the FBI's investigative priority. The last few years have also included an adjustment of personnel assignments and an identified need for scientists, language specialists, and computer experts. September 11 presented demands that went far and above the means of individual agencies. Within the Bureau itself and among law enforcemcent agencies nationwide, disaster called for an automatic need to work together toward a single mission of safety. It called for new behavior within the parochial halls of the FBI. The FBI met those challenges head-on, but not without some criticism.

In the wake of the disaster, the FBI began 24/7 activity of personnel all over the world. Damage assessment of the attacks, carried out at a rapid pace, was under intense scrutiny.

FBI Director Mueller immediately dedicated the FBI to its current top two priorities: protect the United States from terrorist attacks and protect the United States against foreign intelligence operations and espionage. This dramatically changed the operations serving the former priorities of drugs and violent crimes. The FBI was criticized in some circles for leaving local task forces up in the air as agents were re-assigned to terrorism, especially those dealing with fugitives, drugs, and bank robberies.

However, prior to September 11, the FBI had been sending personnel overseas. The FBI was a principle in creating the Budapest Academy, through which increased cooperation was forged with overseas authorities. Global urgency revealed itself time and again in stolen art, drug, and organized crime matters. The FBI sent Disaster Teams and Evidence Response Teams abroad at the behest of Presidents Clinton and Bush as a sign of cooperation in the face of mass graves in Bosnia and Kosovo, as well as in the arrests of high profile FBI terrorist subjects.

So working cases of this nature was not entirely new territory to the FBI. It was not the norm, but it was evolving as FBI turf. The distinction now is that the work is shared with other government agencies under a nationwide spotlight.

Perhaps the post-September 11 changes in the FBI are felt most strongly in its culture. The FBI has always been known as fedora-wearing gangbusters, untouchables, white shirted, pin-stripe suited men with unequaled skill and integrity. But the diversity of personnel and purpose have changed since Hoover's death in 1972, and September 11 is the window through which the country can see the evolving FBI. Already more diversified in personnel, expertise, and specialized missions than before, the FBI continues to create a record of excellence. The Bureau faces an increased complexity of investigative matters, and an ever-growing influence of technology on both crime and its detection. The biggest change, however, is dealing with the absolute scrutiny of American citizens regarding the attacks. There have been several commissions and Congressional inquires attempting to identify the deficiencies that contributed to the disaster; America is unsettled about a security it once took for granted. Since 9/11, the FBI has become more open about internal issues and corrections.

It is impossible to assess, until more time has passed, how much the FBI's legacy will be affected.

PART THREE

Career Opportunities with the FBI

CHAPTER

Applicant Outlook

The FBI has a strong commitment to equal opportunity employment, and as you will see, the Bureau has developed a very strict, but fair, selection process. All applicants are given an equal opportunity, consistent with established rules and procedures, to compete for vacancies within the Bureau. Historically, there has not been much turnover in the Bureau—the overall attrition rate for FBI employees, including retirements, has been only five percent.

The FBI has always sought to hire based on the "needs of the Bureau." Since its mission turned on a dime on September 11, personnel needs have shifted in order to address the numerous changes. In the last four years, there has been what the *LA Times* news service calls "an exodus from the ranks of the FBI." Within a 24-month period, the *LA Times* reported the top terrorism position changed hands five times. Over 1,300 agents, or 10 percent of the agent population, were eligible to retire in 2002. As a result, the FBI is currently in a hiring mode. Many executives, agents, and analysts have left for other agency posts or to go into private consultancy or the private sector. In 2004, the Bureau had a plan to hire 400 new analysts, given the increased importance of intelligence and the broad mission of counterterrorism.

WHAT THE FBI IS LOOKING FOR

Let's consider some of the numbers. The FBI has over 80,000 applications currently in review. The average age of new agent hires is 31, which translates to several years of work and life experience. The majority of applicants who receive appointments also have a minimum of a Master's degree.

When making decisions, the FBI is going to give a long look to the following qualifications and expertise:

- former military or police experience
- language abilities—especially Middle Eastern and Arab dialects, not to mention any of the emerging Soviet state languages
- computer science expertise
- scientists
- analysts

The above is not an exclusive list, but it addresses some of the most identifiable personnel needs of the current Bureau. These positions are both agent and professional staff; equally important to the work of the FBI. Read more about the demands of each position in chapters 7 and 8.

Today's Bureau needs individuals who are intelligent, flexible, mature, and capable of interacting with collegues from agencies abroad and at home. We have entered a new era in policing. The 1970s spoke of professionalization. The new century demands teamwork and the pooling of expertise toward the common goal of American security both home and abroad.

DIVERSITY

The Bureau isn't looking to fill quotas. It is a need of patriots of all abilitites and vision. The Bureau's integrity, character, and excellence comes to it through its personnel. The FBI simply identifies talent and strength, hones it, and directs it to the greatest need.

The role of the FBI's Office of Equal Employment Opportunity Affairs is to provide equal opportunity in employment for all persons; to prohibit discrimination in employment because of race, color, religion, sex, national origin, sexual orientation, age, or handicap; and to promote the full realization of equal employment opportunity through a continuing affirmative action program.

The following charts show a breakdown of FBI employees by gender and race:

EMPLOYEE STATISTICS

Special Agent Employment Statistics as of 6/30/03

	No. of Men	% of Total	No. of Women	% of Total	Total Group	% of Total
Am. Indian	37	.3	11	.1	48	.4
Asian	311	2.7	59	.5	370	3.2
Black	518	4.5	125	1.1	643	5.5
Hispanic	709	6.1	150	1.3	859	7.4
White	7,949	68.3	1,764	15.2	9,713	83.5
TOTALS	9,524	81.9	2,109	18.1	11,633	100

Support Personnel Employment Statistics as of 6/30/03

	No. of Men	% of Total	No. of Women	% of Total	Total Group	% of Total
Am. Indian	32	.2	55	.3	87	.5
Asian	183	1.2	226	1.4	408	2.6
Black	631	4.0	2,827	17.8	3,458	21.7
Hispanic	272	1.7	605	3.8	877	5.5
White	4,144	26.1	6,930	43.6	11,074	69.6
TOTALS	5,262	33.1	10,642	66.9	15,904	100

Note: Due to rounding of figures, these totals might not be exact to the tenth.
All information obtained from www.fbi.gov.

SALARY

Unlike most government agencies, the FBI does its own hiring. But the pay and promotion standards correspond to government guidelines. In the descriptions of specific job requirements, you will see mentions of levels on government pay scales, such as GS 14. Take a look at the pay scale charts starting on page 263 to see the pay scale range for the levels mentioned.

RETIREMENT

The FBI has a retirement program different from many non-law enforcement federal agencies. The FBI holds you may retire at age 50, with at least 20 years of service. Mandatory retirement age for agents is currently 65; many have pushed to have it elevated to 67.

FBI Online

The FBI has recently set up an Employment Home Page as part of its website at www.fbi.gov. There, you can look up job postings in all areas of the Bureau, check out job requirements, and download an application form. The FBI also employs agents and support professionals with disabilities. Direct contact with the FBI can provide the specific details involving the parameters of such employment.

CHAPTER

Special Agent Positions

The FBI Special Agents are without a doubt the most visible members of the FBI. While it has always been pretty tough to receive an appointment as an FBI agent, it has become especially competitive over the past few years. I'm saying this not to be discouraging, but to be realistic. "When I came in, one in 400 was appointed to the Academy," says Special Agent Jim McFall. "Now it's one in a thousand. The winnowing process is very, very thorough. Very objective, but very thorough."

These are the minimum qualifications for Special Agents, and I stress minimum. If you don't meet all these criteria, there's no way you'll get into the Bureau as a Special Agent. That's just a fact.

- You must be a U.S. citizen, or a citizen of Northern Mariana Islands.
- You must be at least 23 years old and no more than 37 years old when you apply.
- You must be completely available for assignment anywhere in the FBI's geographic jurisdiction.
- You must hold a valid driver's license.
- You must have a degree from a four-year resident program at an accredited college that is certified by one of the six regional accrediting bodies of the Commission of Institutions of Higher Education.

- You must be deemed by the FBI's Chief Medical Officer to be physically able to enage in firearms use, raids, defensive tactics, and other essential job functions.

AUTOMATIC DISQUALIFIERS

The following list of incidents will automatically disqualify you from Special Agent consideration:

- conviction of a felony
- use of illegal drugs

  The FBI is firm about a drug free society and workplace. It is unlawful for FBI employees to use drugs, and any use will not be tolerated. The FBI does not condone any prior unlawful drug use by applicants. The following is the criteria for any applicant with past drug use:

  — If you were once employed in law enforcement or as a prosecutor are proven to have used illegal drugs, you will be found unsuitable.

  — If you have misrepresented your drug history, you will be found unsuitable.

  — If you have sold drugs for a profit at any time, you will be found unsuitable.

  — If you have used any illegal drugs (including anabolic steroids after February 1991) other than marijuana within the past 10 years or more than five times in your life, you will be found unsuitable.

  — If you have used marijuana within the past three years or more than 15 times in your life, you will be found unsuitable.

  This policy is non-negotiable. Many applicants think they can clean up their history. I advise you not to try. Your lack of candor will be viewed as a more serious lack of integrity. It is what it is. You made these decisions … you have to live with them.

- default of student loan insured by U.S. government
- failure of urinalysis drug test, or
- failure to register with the Selective Service System

SPECIAL AGENT ENTRY PROGRAMS

The FBI puts new Special Agents into four categories, or "entry programs," depending on the qualifications the candidates bring to the job. The mix of entry programs within any one new agents' class varies, depending on what the Bureau needs at a particular time.

Law

Those entering in this program have a J.D. degree from an accredited resident law school. You don't necessarily have to have passed a state bar exam, although it can't hurt.

There are two reasons why a law degree is a desirable asset. First, if you're going to enforce the federal laws, you should have an appreciation and understanding of the Federal Rules of Criminal Procedure. Second, the analytical training you get in law school will help you identify the elements of a criminal violation and collect the evidence needed for successful prosecution.

Accounting

Special Agents in the accounting program hold a B.S. degree with a major in accounting or a related discipline, and they must be eligible to take the CPA examination. If you haven't passed the CPA exam before you apply, you must pass the FBI's accounting test.

An accounting degree is a desirable asset because Special Agents often need to trace financial transactions and analyze complex accounting records. Training in accounting and experience with financial systems will help an investigator develop relevant evidence to uncover sophisticated financial crimes. Special Agent accountants often testify in such white-collar crime cases as expert witnesses, and need to be accredited as financial experts.

Language

Your B.S. or B.A. can be in any discipline, and you must be able to demonstrate proficiency in a language that meets the needs of the FBI. Those languages shift from year to year, depending on factors as varied as international crime patterns and Bureau retirement rates.

By the way, "proficiency" doesn't mean being able to ask directions and order a beer. The tests administered by the FBI require you to be fluent in speaking, writing, and translating. You will need to pass a proficiency exam under this entry program.

Diversified

You must hold a B.S. or B.A. in any discipline and have at least three years of full-time work experience. If you have an advanced degree, you need a minimum of two years of full-time work experience.

The diversified entry program covers everyone from police officers to soldiers to psychologists to teachers. It's impossible to tell what specific careers will meet the needs of the FBI at any particular point.

SPECIAL AGENT RECRUITING

I want to put a word in here about the way the FBI recruits for Special Agents. Supervisory Special Agent Doug Rhoads, who designed the current program, will describe it in some detail later in the chapter. But I want to just express my own opinion here.

These days, anytime you talk about diversity in the work force, people start thinking—or talking—about quotas and reverse discrimination. I've had people tell me about a nephew of theirs who was a Marine captain and a homicide detective in New York City and has a black belt in karate and wrestles alligators in his spare time and is just all around rough and tough, and he couldn't get into the FBI because he's a white male, while they are letting in all these women and minorities who can't do what he can do.

Well, the fact is the Bureau needs more than alligator wrestlers. Take a look at all the different kinds of cases the Bureau handles. You can't tackle a range of investigations that broad without diversity of skills, diversity of approaches, and diversity of talents.

Yes, there are going to be intelligent, talented, hard-working white men who don't make it into the FBI. There are also going to be intelligent, talented, hard-working women, Asians, Hispanics, African Americans, and Native Americans who don't make it in. The process is just too competitive to include everyone who might possibly be a good agent. But I honestly believe, and I've seen from my own experience, that the Bureau makes its decisions as fairly and objectively as possible.

I also believe that there's an inherent value in diversity. Remember when Frank Watts talked about how much easier it was for him, as a Southerner, to talk to other Southerners? That holds true for all kinds of groups. You don't have to be a minority to understand or talk to members of a minority, but it doesn't hurt. Often that common ground can help put a nervous or angry witness at ease. Diversity is also more than simply ethnic or racial background—it is also about differing life experiences. The FBI can only operate with individuals of differing racial or regional backgrounds, temperments, and interests. The FBI is about talking to people from every walk of life.

Again, I want to stress that this is just my opinion—not official policy. But some of you reading this are going to apply to the FBI, and you aren't going to get in. I don't want you to think it's because someone less qualified took your place.

DEVELOPMENT OF AN APPLICANT PROGRAM

Since Supervisory Special Agent Doug Rhoads spent almost eight years designing and running the recruiting program, I'm going to let him take over. So here's Doug:

> I'll never forget a futurist saying to me, "If you want to see what the country's going to look like in 20 years, go take a look at the first grade right now." Take a look at any elementary school now, and you'll see that by 2020, white males are not going to be the majority. A law enforcement agency as big as the FBI, as visible as the FBI, has to reflect the culture. Has to.
>
> I was called back to headquarters in 1983 to work on the recruiting program, because William Webster had taken a look ahead. When my group came in—1969 to 1972—that was the biggest hiring era. Now, a lot of these agents were going to retire after 20 years. The issue was, how are you going to replace half the agent workforce in this six-, eight-year window? And how are you going to do it when you rely on self-recruiting?
>
> The old recruiting method was—well, there was no method. There were 58 different field offices with 58 different systems. When there was a big push to hire agents, the Bureau would drop leaflets over Detroit, and everybody looking for a job would come in the door.

There were two problems with that. First, that approach was so broad that it forced the system to deselect hundreds of people. You made 90 percent of your applicants mad because you didn't give them a job.

Second, with that approach you ended up with an overwhelming majority of white male agents with a modified background. And the fact was, you didn't have to recruit those guys. They grew up like me, always wanting to be a Fed. That group always self-recruits. The FBI could do all its hiring out of that group alone and never have to worry.

But I give Director Webster credit for thinking ahead. Whatever other faults he and the people around him may have had, they were very creative in planning for the Bureau's future.

Take a simple thing like keyboard skills. When I joined the Bureau, computers were nowhere. Now you can't function without them. You don't have to be a computer whiz, but you have to have a basic level of comfort, just to get the job done. And you will need some people who are computer whizzes (scientists).

So the people at headquarters said, "You know, we're going to need people who know about computers. We're going to need more people with language skills." Fifteen years ago, Farsi wasn't a necessary language. Today it is.

Fifteen years ago, Spanish was common, but not like it is today. In five states—California, Florida, Texas, Illinois, and New York—a lot of the language spoken is Spanish. You've got to have Spanish-speaking agents, and not because Spanish speakers are more likely to be criminals. How do you go do a routine background check in Harlingen, Texas, or an investigation in Nogales, New Mexico, when you don't have any Spanish speakers?

We decided we need bilingual agents, we need agents with financial advising skills. We need these different skills. Where are we going to find them? I always stress to the recruiters that you've got to get out of your culture.

I did a survey of new agents for about a year. I was trying to see where they were coming from. White males were still a predominant piece of the hiring, and when you asked what attracted them to the Bureau, where did they first learn about the Bureau, all of them said something like "lifelong goal," "contact with an onboard Special Agent," "contact with a law enforcement official who knew an onboard agent." Just about 100 percent had personal contact with an agent.

Now, when you looked at women, that wasn't true. It could have been advertising, it could have been a career day at their college. When you looked at minorities, same thing. They saw an ad in Black Enterprise Magazine, or they went to a special minority recruiting event.

That extends to the professions as well. How do you think an electrical engineer knows the Bureau wants him? Or someone who's proficient in Farsi, or Urdu, or any other language the Bureau might need? If you want those kinds of folks to do those diverse kinds of things you need, targeted advertising and targeted outreach is a part of it, like or not.

When I went back to Headquarters in 1983, I was assigned to the Administrative Services division, on the personnel side. There I was, by myself, one person to design this thing. I just put on a coat and tie and showed up and said, "Well, what are we going to do here?"

As I jumped in I was very impressed with everyone at the Bureau. Even though there's a human resistance to change, nobody—from the highest levels of management to the agents on the street—nobody ever tried to do anything other than a good job. There was resistance to change, and yet in the end people like to do the right thing.

From 1983 to 1985 was the planning stage. Eventually my office became a unit, the Personnel Resources Unit, with three or four agents assigned to it along with five or six support personnel. It's evolved so that pure

recruitment is the second half of it. The main
purpose of the unit is to plan for the future.
What do you need? When are you going to need it?
How many people are you losing each year? How
many retire, how many are fired, how many
resign? What were these people doing?

It's the front end, the planning, that makes
the recruitment work. If you need computer
people next year, don't be dropping those
leaflets over Detroit. Figure out what these
people read, put an ad in there, and make the FBI
a career option for computer experts. If you
think you're going to need computer people in
three, four, five years, go to the schools. Talk
to your current people, find out where they
went, what schools they recommend. You may only
need to do that for a couple of years, then you
can shift your focus.

As far as recruiting itself, we developed a
coherent system across the country. Each
division has an Applicant Coordinator, who's the
agent designated to set up the interviews,
coordinate the background checks, and go to
career recruiting events in his or her
respective territory. Some of these Applicant
Coordinators were very effective. They enjoyed
what they were doing, they got support from
their Special Agent in Charge. Others didn't
want the job; they wanted to be out working

criminal cases, they got stuck with this job,
for whatever reason.

Certain divisions did very well, much better
than others, based on pure numbers. No one was
unhappy with the quality of the agents
recruited; it's just that some offices brought
you a bigger pool to choose from. Say a big
office like Miami brought in five, while a
little office like Tampa hired 50. Well, what's
Tampa doing that Miami isn't?

I brought together all the Tampas, everyone
whose program was working well. Everyone talked
about what they were doing, and we analyzed it.
Then we had a series of conferences, five around
the country, brought all the recruiters together
and let these people who were doing it well talk
about what they did. Everybody left, then we
analyzed the program again, and started to give
a national direction. That was Phase I.

Phase II to was get recruiters out of their
own cultures. I had every recruiter get involved
with his or her own local or regional college
placement association. There's an actual
structured association in every state and every
region of the country that brings together
corporate business people who are recruiting
college graduates. People would say, "No, you
can't do that. The Bureau doesn't hire new

graduates. We only hire people with three years'
work experience."

Well, the bottom line is, that's a funnel
they pass through. How are you going to reach
them once they leave the campus? You're back to
dropping leaflets over Detroit. Pick 150
colleges, have recruiters go there, and sell the
FBI. If you make a good impression, the person
that goes to work for a big accounting firm, does
well, decides a few years later he wants a career
change—he'll remember that guy from the FBI.

Or the top performer at that accounting firm
remembers the FBI recruiter at career day. She
doesn't want to leave, but she has lunch with a
co-worker, someone talented and bright who wants
a change. She says, "Why don't you try the FBI?"
Each person has a sphere of influence, and you
want to intersect as many spheres as you can,
whether it's through campus visits, professional
associations, or just the contacts you make
going about your job as an agent.

The current applicant program continues to adjust to the present personnel
needs of the FBI. Given the enormous number of applicants, the criteria for
selection rarely ends up being the minimum advertised standards. The
median standards are raised by the very nature and characteristics of this
applicant pool. The FBI works to make this process fair.

THE BASICS: SPECIAL AGENT SKILLS

The application process is mutually beneficial. The FBI gets a good look at you, and you get a better look at the FBI as an employer. There are particular attributes associated with a successful agent; some you can teach and others you can't. Let's discuss both.

Intrinsic Qualities

You develop these qualitites as you mature and live a thorough life: perseverance, flexibility, courage, intelligence, tenacity, and other characteristics valuable to a career involving discretion and authority involving deadly force. No one can teach you what you learn from experience. This is one of the main reasons the FBI looks for work and life experience, and why the median age for current applicants is 31. For example, what does pursuit of a graduate degree tell an employer about you? It describes your ability to handle multiple responsibilities; it describes your perseverance, and it suggests a pursuit of excellence. I might add again that the median level of education for applicants is a Master's degree. An employer like the FBI wants to be able to predict to some degree your ability to handle stress and make cogent decisions at the same time.

Extrinsic Qualitites

Extrinsic qualities might be height, weight, phsyical fitness, and the ability to speak confidently and carry yourself in a professional manner. Some of these qualities are taught and stressed in training, and some you are expected to develop throughout your career. The application process, directly or indirectly, screens for people with talent in these areas. Be cognizant of these skills and you will be better prepared for the process. These are also good skills you can put to use in any profession.

Interrogation Skills

This can be one of the most interesting, rewarding aspects of the job. Interrogation is about reading a person who sits in front of you. It is about observation using verbal and non-verbal cues; about physical gestures and movements. In many cases, you get only one chance to make an assessment. Every subject is different, and you have to be able to read the situation and respond on the fly. Like most things, interrogation only gets easier with experience. Here are a few guidelines for success:

Do your homework. Bob McGonigel describes his experience: "At times, particularly in typical organized crime cases, my supervisor would suggest, 'Well, go see him. He'll talk to you.' And I would just not do it. Because if I didn't know enough about the case, and the individual, and the other players—that would become apparent to the person I was trying to interrogate, and I wouldn't even know enough to call them on a lie. You're just exhibiting your ignorance. And that's the worst thing you can do."

Look for the weak spot. Just as you don't want to reveal your own weakness to the subject, you're trying to discover and exploit his weaknesses. This is how Special Agent Phil Grivas describes it: "You have to try to find where they're vulnerable, an Achilles heel. You may say, 'Oh—you got two little kids? How old do you think they're going to be when you see them again? You're never going to be with them through most of their formative years. You're never going to go out and play baseball. You come out, your kids are going to be 20, 25 years old.' You try to find something. Sometimes you gotta play a little bit of hardball. 'You ever been in jail before? You know what they do to good-looking guys like you? It's not gonna be fun. You really want to put that many years in there? What do you think you're going to be like when you come out?' Everybody has a chord you can strike, and if you find it, you'll get to them. They'll look at what they've done, and what their prospects really are. And they'll start talking."

Look for common ground. It will sometimes surprise you how much common ground there is. You need to find it and use it to humanize yourself and the victims you're working for. Establishing a connection with the subject can make the difference between getting the information you need and getting stonewalled. Phil Grivas says, "The people who commit the most horrendous crimes—I mean rape, and child murder, mutilation, forget about it—when these people are away from that element, away from that crime of opportunity scenario, many of these people are John Q. Average. They like the same teams you do. Or they grew up in the same neighborhood you did. They're very average. It's just that they get caught up with these people, and the drugs, and this and that. And next thing you know they're doing things they never dreamed that they could."

Control the situation. Always keep in mind that you are running the show—and run it. Make sure you are in charge of everything that goes on throughout the interrogation. You may or may not want to demonstrate that control. That's part of the unpredictability of interrogations. Phil Grivas describes some of his control techniques. "Let's say we've got a subject locked up, and we think he'd respond better to somebody at a higher rank, as opposed to an agent. I'd have somebody introduce me as the inspector from Washington, up in New York to personally oversee this investigation. I'd be sitting there, with my jacket on, and people would come in and give me these very important documents to sign—just a blank sheet of paper, but he doesn't know that. Someone would come in: 'Mr. Grivas, there's a phone call for you from Washington.' I'd say, 'I'm busy with this gentleman now, just give me a minute.' So all of a sudden, the guy looks at you differently. Now, when you tell the subject, 'Look, you want to help yourself? You better talk to me'—well, he might take you a little more seriously."

There are no absolutes. Whatever rules you learn, you have to be prepared to throw them out the window if the situation requires it. In the 1970s, Bob McGonigel became involved with the investigation of a major kidnapping, and had to take over a suspect interview with no preparation. "I was working in the command post when the call came in, that they had retrieved the victim, and they were bringing two subjects in. One of the supervisors asked me to interview one of the subjects. Initially, I felt a little overwhelmed, because I didn't know that much about the details. And the interview lasted, unfortunately, 16 hours. He was lying in the beginning, denying it. And then he gave us a confession that was ridiculous. And we kind of threw that one aside, and kept after him. In the end, he gave us a confession that was enough ultimately to convict him. I was proud of the fact that I was thrown into the gap, with no preparation, and came through."

Always ask some questions you already know the answers to. When possible, have some questions you already know the answers to, so you can gauge a subject's degree of truthfulness. Understand this—subjects will never tell you everything…usually only enough to get through their current circumstances or as much as they believe can manipulate the discussion in their favor.

Surveillance Skills

Bob McGonigel was great at surveillance. Here's what he said on the topic:

"The challenge is first, making sure you don't get made, and second, accomplishing the objective—obtaining the information you need. That information could be used to prosecute the subjects, or it could be used to show that these people aren't doing anything illegal. Maybe when a suspect is put under surveillance, you'll find out that they're not involved in it at all. It's a dead end, and you have to redirect.

"I loved surveillance. For a while, I was in what they call "Special Operations." Anywhere from four to seven agents who would work together in concert, basically the top-notch cases. We'd start on surveillance, but in the end we doing most of the arrests in those cases also. We had some very unusual vehicles, cars that had been seized by the government, including a Ferrari, which was virtually useless as a surveillance vehicle. When we wanted to go into a neighborhood, we'd send in a female agent in the Ferrari, just have her drive around, and park different places. People would all look toward her, and no one noticed us at all."

Janet Engle also had a gift for surveillance.

"I agree with what SA McGonigal says about surveillance. It is a challenge and an opportunity for agents to play key roles. Women were often considered simply "bracelets." Let me explain."Bracelets" means you don't say anything. You are there to be on a male agent's arm and observe. In the early days, it also meant you weren't expected to have an opinion or interact as a situation developed. But that has also changed. Also, a couple sitting in a vehicle was less suspicious than two men or two women. You could design a team to fit the environment.

"You will find agents have very different personalities and it is important as a team leader to know those strengths and make use of them, regardless of whether one is male or female. And so maybe these days, it may be time to send some guy in to just "look good," wouldn't you say? Can you tell I believe a sense of humor is invaluable. It is a part of the comraderie I so enjoyed on this job.

"As a team leader, it was my responsibility to understand the baseline behavior and movements of subjects in order to identify the departures in those routines important to detailing criminal behavior. I was responsible for my team having current information and the tools to do that job. Documenting a surveillance was vital for a case to succeed. Attention to details and nuances were critcal to observe and record. The paper is vital. If you don't record it properly, it didn't happen.

"Surveillance also helped identify subjects not previously associated with the target. The 24/7 surveillance can be very difficult, but very rich in information. First, 24/7 coverage is not anticipated by most people and often reveals important information on predicting possible future movements."

The Ability to Write Reports

Writing skills are essential in the Bureau. You don't have to be Shakespeare, but you need to have a handle on the basics, meaning spelling, grammar, and organization of ideas. These reports are used by the FBI and a vast number of other agencies or offices. Every report you write represents you as a professional and the FBI as an agency. There are no excuses for careless errors. Janet Engle recalls part of her applicant exams was a spelling test; all terms tested were terms commonly used within the Bureau.

Just about any investigation, no matter how minor, almost immediately turns into something that looks like a recycling bin—forensic reports, interview transcripts, crime scene descriptions, background reports, legal briefs, phone messages, more bits of paper than you can believe. You have to be able to assemble all that information, read it and synthesize it, identify the critical points, organize them logically, and present the relevant material and your conclusions clearly and concisely. Clarity, logic, completeness—those are the critical factors in writing up a report.

This is how Jim McFall puts it: "There's an old saying—'You write a report to express, not impress.' Reports are not rated by how much they weigh—although I've seen some that ran several volumes. But if I took one of my reports and handed it to you, you could read it from front to back and know exactly what the case was about. You'd know what the alleged violation was, you'd know who the witnesses were, the subjects, the empirical data that was obtained—it's all there." As another FBI agent told me "If it's not on paper, it didn't happen." Being out on the street is great, but our job is to reduce it to writing and a prosecutable case.

The Ability to Give Testimony

You are going to have to communicate orally, as well as on paper. When you are called to give testimony, as an investigator or as an expert witness, you have to be able to express yourself clearly and confidently without letting the opposing counsel rattle you. You also need to make sure your point gets across to the jury, and that your information is presented in a manner comprehensible to a cross-section of citizens.

Bruce Koenig describes what can happen when you've got someone who thinks a bit too much of himself up on the stand:

"I haven't seen it really in the FBI at all. But I have seen some of these Ph.D.'s get up on the stand and actually laugh at a prosecutor's question. They'll literally laugh and say, "I can't answer that question. There's nobody in this courtroom smart enough to understand my answer." They don't understand what a negative impact that has on the jury. Everyone on that jury thinks, "What a pompous idiot." That just hurts the prosecution.

"I believe part of my job is to give people some understanding of audio tapes. This is my little stage, my chance to get up there and explain to them exactly what a tape is and how the tape recorder works. I give them the basics before we get into the complicated stuff. I can't expect them to know all that I know, but I can certainly educate them enough so they can comprehend what I tell them. That's vital."

Testifying in a trial can also be tremendously rewarding. After all your work, you finally have a chance to face the criminal in court and, you hope, help put him away. Greg Cooper describes one of these experiences:

"I was contacted by one of the people at VICAP, who said, "'I've got these two cases out of North Carolina. Two separate jurisdictions. I've talked to both county attorneys, and they don't feel that they can successfully convict this guy of either case without being able to introduce evidence linking both cases. They want to do it from a behavioral perspective, and I don't think there's anything there.

"Of course, he was looking at it from a different perspective. He wasn't a profiler, which was why he came to our unit. I take a look at the cases, two incredibly vicious murders, and then I call the prosecutors. I say, 'I think we can link these cases together by some of the unique behavior here.'

"They're very, very excited, because they feel now they might have a shot at getting this guy. I review the cases, analyze them, go to North Carolina to testify. Carl Steven Mosley is the defendant.

"The experience was so dramatic. The courtroom is filled with people, the public, and the media, but everyone's totally silent. Just listening. As I'm testifying, I look eye to eye with Mosley, and he has a look on his face like, 'How the hell did you know? How do you know all this?'

"He was convicted and sentenced to death. Then, ten months later, I went back and testified in the second trial. One day, one of the deputies told me that he'd escorted Mosely into court that day. When Mosely saw me, he said, 'There's the son of a bitch who's gonna try to make them think I did this one, too.' I just smiled and told the deputy, 'That's exactly right.'

"At this point, profiling was still fairly new. I think John was the only person who'd been accepted as an expert witness in this area, so I felt a certain amount of pressure. But there was no doubt in my mind that Mosely had committed both murders.

"The defense attorneys were really rattled. They were so overwhelmed, just flustered. They didn't know what questions to ask. They became very, very upset that this evidence was even allowed. They appealed the conviction based specifically on my testimony, saying it shouldn't have been allowed.

"The case has gone through two different appeals processes—state and federal level. But the convictions have been upheld.

"I'm glad I helped put Mosely away. I just wish they could bring him back to carry out the second execution."

Testifying is about knowing your case and organizing the facts in such a way as to support the prosecution's theory of the crime. The training academy has used a moot court project in order to give agents in training some experience.

SPECIAL AGENT CAREER PATHS

The FBI does not expect every agent to take an up-or-out career path. You can climb through the ranks, like Phil Grivas and Rodney Davis, or you can spend your career on the front lines, like Janet Engle and Bob McGonigel. The Bureau values experience and expertise, no matter where the individual chooses to exercise it.

In the current Bureau climate, there are no rules. An FBI Agent or Support Professional serves at the whims of the Director. Terrorism and other Bureau missions have everything to do with the Director's application of both personnel expertise and other resources. Although there may be "programs" in place regarding assignment, the Director may dictate otherwise.

Generally, all new agents serve a two-year probationary period. After graduation from the Academy, a new Special Agent is assigned to an FBI field office, based on the Bureau's needs. You can ask for a particular posting, but there's no guarantee you will get it. Generally, new agents stay in their first offices of assignment for four years.

Those years give the new agent a chance to get some real-world experience. You'll probably start out on the more straightforward cases such as bank robbery or fugitive investigations. This lets you get the hands-on experience you'll need in the basics of investigation. You'll also start to realize what kinds of work you're drawn to—it might be organized crime, white-collar crime, or forensics. But those first years are a great opportunity to do some frontline, crime-fighting work. These first years also represent a time to become familiar with the way the job is done: the paperwork, interagency relations, and "paying dues." Believe me when I tell you, new agents (no matter how impressive the resumé) need to adjust to the FBI and its work. Take advantage of experienced agents, keep your ego in check, and learn the job. Don't worry, your talents will be noticed. "Time on the job" is an important element of credibility in the law enforcement culture.

When you reach that four or five year mark, you're considered eligible for what's called "a nonvoluntary rotational transfer," which means you'll be sent to another office, again depending on the needs of the FBI. However, Special Agents who stay in an office for more than ten years generally will not be considered for a nonvoluntary rotational transfer. Transfers are largely about budget and personnel needs. Transfers currently occur more infrequently than in the past. Speciality transfers are more prevalent. Avail yourself of whatever specialty training you are able. It simply broadens the posssibility of your assignments.

Specialties

The question I'm asked, over and over, is, "How do I get to be a profiler?" The fact is that profiling, and every other specialty within the FBI, isn't something you just step right into. For any specialty, you have to begin by establishing a good record as an investigator at your first few postings. Attend the relevant in-service classes back at the Academy, and do well at those. There may be particular assignments you need to handle for a few years before you'll be considered. For instance, Greg Cooper had to put in a stint as a NCAVC coordinator before he could apply for the profiling unit.

Once you've met all the requirements for the specialty, you still have to go through at least one year of training. It's fascinating, but it's not easy. Greg describes what is was like when he finally made it back to Quantico as a profiler:

"The first thing that happened was training for a year. You have this unbelievable experience, both academically and practically, because you are assigned to cases right away. So I'm taking classes at the National Academy in interpersonal violence and death investigations, classes at the Institute of

Pathology, Psychology and Law at the University of Virginia. It's this intensive immersion—no matter what your experience has been before, this totally takes it to another level. The learning curve is phenomenal. And it's not quite like any other academic experience, because you have an opportunity to immediately apply the things you're learning. You're working cases right away and you are learning from those you're working with at the same time.

"It's unbelievably high-pressure, and unbelievably rewarding. You have the benefit of academics and of working the case with people who have already developed abilities and you share insights as they guide you.; it's a tremendous experience."

SPECIAL AGENT PAY SCALE

Special Agents enter as GS 10 at $42,548 when they enter the Academy, and can advance to GS 13 in field assignments (turn to page 264 to view a chart detailing General Schedule salaries and levels). Promotions to supervisory, management, and executive positions are available in Grades 14 and 15, as well as in the Senior Executive Service. Most senior investigators, depending on the Division assignment, make close to or over $100,000.

In some areas—New York City and Los Angeles, for example—agents receive a "locality adjustment." This is a percentage added to the base pay, to make up for the increased cost of living in those areas.

Special Agents are required to be available for duty 24 hours a day. Therefore, they're also provided with availability pay—equal to 25 percent of an agent's total salary, which includes base salary plus any locality adjustment.

In 1980, FBI Agents created a professional organization known as the FBI Agents' Association. This organization, which currently involves a considerable majority of on-board agents, acts similarly to a union (though it does not have contract bargaining powers, as agents do not have a contract such

221

as most police departments). However, this body is an effective lobby for agents' pay and other important work-related issues. It is a vital body of both information and support for FBI Agents.

CHAPTER

Professional Support Positions

Professional Support personnel have an illustrious history with the FBI. Their collective contributions are well known to all FBI employees; support professionals literally organized and ran offices in the Bureau's infancy, as bosses changed and agents were transferred. Support professionals were the constancy in these divisions. Their positions and contributions have only increased and accelerated the competency of the Bureau. Professional staff positions are not simply "clerical," as described in the early years of the FBI. Some positions are administrative, while others are technological and scientific. All are integral to the FBI mission. The Special Agents couldn't do their jobs without excellent contributions from other collegueas at the FBI. These people's backgrounds, and the jobs they do, cover a tremendous range. Professional Support positions now range from armed specialized surveillance units to scientists and engineers for the highly complex FBI Laboratory and its Advanced Engineering Research Section located at Quantico, Virginia.

Supervisory Special Agent Jim O'Connor says, "Criminal justice is a multidisciplinary, interdisciplinary field. For instance, investigators learn a lot from journalists. Where do I go for sources? What are the sources of information that are legal?" One of the strengths of the FBI is that it does not limit applicants to any one degree. The broader the educational backgrounds in an agency, the more capable the agency is going to be. Say I have a government fraud case, and it happens to involve a highway construction project. I need engineers to understand what the specifications were, whether the construction met those specs. And that's just one example. The FBI specifically recruits and focuses on areas that broaden its capabilities. And so the FBI favors lawyers and accountants, but also linguists, scientists, computer scientists, and behavioral scientists. Firearms experts, security, and engineers are also important positions.

PROFESSIONAL POSITIONS

This category covers job descriptions ranging from attorneys, to personnel psychologists, to contract specialists, and more. A few Professional Support positions (for instance, Investigative Specialist) require employees to be available both for transfer or temporary duty assignments—wherever the needs of the FBI dictate. However, most Professional Support positions don't require this willingness to pick up and go. These positions require background investigations identical to those of the agent position, buthere are no exams or entrance medical information. There is no mandatory retirement age for most Professional Support positions.

Just as an example, here are the job description and minimum requirements for one professional job—a biologist/forensic examiner.

Sample Job Description: Biologist/Forensic Examiner

General Duties

These folks are responsible for planning, coordinating, directing, and conducting forensic science activities in the FBI Lab. This includes inventory duties on samples; examining and performing comprehensive technical analyses of evidence such as DNA in body tissues, fluids, and body fluid stains; forensic serology of blood and other body fluids; and locating, identifying, reconstructing and preserving pertinent items of evidence for examination from crime scenes. As with Special Agents who are forensic specialists, forensic examiners also prepare and furnish oral and written reports and testify in court as necessary.

General Qualifications

Applicants must have at least a Bachelor's degree in biochemistry, biological sciences, biotechnology or a related discipline. Your transcript must include a minimum of 24 semester hours in biochemistry or the biological sciences.

The pay for forensic examiners ranges from GS 7 to GS 13, depending on experience (turn to page 264 to view the GS chart of salaries).

Qualifications for GS 7: One full year of graduate-level education, superior academic achievement in one of the above disciplines, or a bachelor's degree and one year of specialized experience in one of the above disciplines.

Qualifications for GS 11: Three full yearsf progressively higher graduate-level education, a Ph.D. or an equivalent doctoral degree, or a Bachelor's degree and one year of specialized experience equivalent to at least GS 9 in the federal service. (Qualifications for GS 12 and GS 13 are similar.)

Special Working Conditions

- Must successfully complete training necessary for certification as an FBI Forensic Examiner.
- Must be willing to work irregular and odd-hour shifts and weekends when necessary.
- Must be willing to work under hazardous conditions in a laboratory that may include regular, recurring exposure to hazardous materials, toxic substances, and blood-borne pathogens.
- Must be willing to travel frequently, usually on short notice, to conduct crime-scene examinations and to testify in court.

- Must be able to lift heavy objects (50 lbs. or more) and have visual acuity to distinguish colors, sizes, and details.

ADMINISTRATIVE SUPPORT POSITIONS

Administrative support positions offer skilled support for investigations. These positions include computer specialists, management analysts, and language specialists.

As an example, we'll take a look at the job description of an intelligence research specialist.

Sample Job Description: Intelligence Research Specialist

General Duties

Employees in this position are responsible for examining and interpreting national security information gathered by the FBI. Intelligence Research Specialists offer support to the counterintelligence, criminal intelligence, counterterrorism, and organized crime missions of the FBI by preparing strategic and operational analyses, developing espionage case studies, and creating threat assessments. These documents are distributed within the FBI, as well as the law enforcement and U.S. intelligence communities.

General Qualifications

Education: There is no specific degree requirement, but your transcript should show coursework in intelligence or intelligence-related disciplines such as history, political science, international affairs, economics, or journalism.

General experience: Your work experience should demonstrate your ability to do the following:

- Analyze problems, identifying significant factors, gathering pertinent data, and recognizing solutions

- Plan and organize work
- Use good judgment
- Communicate effectively orally and in writing

Specialized experience: The Bureau will look for experience directly related to the position to be filled. This could include, but is not limited to, analytical, research or writing duties associated with drug intelligence, or similar experience in a related discipline such as history, political science, international affairs, economics or journalism.

The pay ranges from GS 5 to GS 14.

Qualifications for GS 5: You must have a Bachelor's degree, or three years of general experience, including one year equivalent to at least GS 4 in the federal service.

Qualifications for GS 11: This requires three full academic years of graduate-level education, or a Ph.D. or equivalent doctoral degree, or one year of specialized experience equivalent to GS 9 in the federal service.

TECHNICAL POSITIONS

These are computer technicians and evidence technicians—the people with more hands-on jobs. They keep the Bureau running, sometimes literally, as in the case of auto technicians.

Sample Job Description: Automotive Technician

Qualifications

Applicants must have a high school diploma or the equivalent, plus work experience.

Pay ranges from W 6 to GS 12, depending on experience.

Duties at W 6: These are basic automotive tasks; mainly routine repairs and maintenance.

Duties at GS 12: This position is officially referred to as the Automotive Program Manager—responsible for managing the garage, equipment, personnel, budget, and the entire automotive fleet at a particular FBI Field Office. The job requires interactions with FBI Special Agents at all levels.

CLERICAL POSITIONS

Bob McGonigel started out on the support staff. He says, "You know, Hoover had a theory—the support people were there to cut down the agents' time in the office, so they could be out doing their work on the street. The Bureau was really run like a computer, before computers existed. We had a highly organized system of filing and indexing, and it really did save the investigators an awful lot of time. You could access information very readily. And now, with computers, the ability to manage information is just tremendous."

That's still the philosophy behind the Bureau's clerical support staff. There are a range of positions available, from evidence technician to squad secretary (the real power). However, the complexity of both the position and the technology have vastly changed the demands of these positions.

PART FOUR
Strategies For Application

CHAPTER

Improving Your Chances

When you apply for a job with the FBI, you are going up against thousands of talented, accomplished people. Only a small percentage of those thousands will make it into the Bureau. How does the FBI make its decisions? Can you do anything to better your chances? This chapter will assist you in that assessment.

No matter what stage of your life you're in—finishing up high school, recently graduated from college, or looking for a career change—the FBI might be a valid career goal for you. But there are several things you should keep in mind before you push ahead.

First, there's no foolproof "recipe" for getting into the FBI, especially as a Special Agent. If you've read this far, you know the Bureau needs people with a variety of backgrounds to handle over 270 statutory categories. But the FBI's specific hiring needs shift from year to year, and so does the pool of applicants. That means no one—not me, not your uncle the former Special Agent, not even your best friend the Applicant Coordinator at the local FBI Field Office—no one can guarantee that your specific package of life experience and skills will get you into the Bureau at a particular point in time. Remember, the latest applicant pool is well over 80,000, with a median age of 31 and a median education background of a Master's degree.

Former military and law enforcement, languages, and the sciences are very attractive backgrounds in today's hiring market.

So before you say "I want to be an FBI Agent," back up a step. Do some profiling on yourself. What, specifically, are you going to do in the FBI? If all you can come up with is "Hang out with Agent Scully and carry a gun," then you've got some serious thinking to do.

Think about the classes in which you succeeded, the activities that absorb you so thoroughly that you lose track of time. Make that area your first career focus. Do not attempt to construct the perfect background. It doesn't exist. Develop a stellar work record. Then, if your skills and experience demonstrate you have what the Bureau needs, you'll have a shot at getting in. And even if you don't get in, you'll still be making a living doing something you enjoy.

This is how Special Agent Owen Smith puts it: "The kind of analysis that's helpful is this: 'What does the FBI want? Which of these things could I enjoy doing?' If you say, 'I don't like doing any of these things, but I'm going to pick one and do it anyhow, so I can be an FBI Agent'—well, I think you're taking a real chance. It may pay off for you, but it's a long shot. You're spending a good part of your life proceeding in that direction, and if it doesn't work out you're in trouble."

So my first piece of advice to you is this: Make joining the FBI a secondary career goal. By all means focus on it, plan for it, let it be one of the factors that determine your educational and life choices. But make sure your primary focus is finding a career that you enjoy, in or out of the FBI.

Keep these in mind as you consider a career working for the FBI:

- 99 percent of what we do is talk to people.
- Today's law enforcement work environment is multiagency and one in which professional respect, cooperation, and sharing expertise is primary.
- Be prepared to pay your dues; have a healthy respect for experience.

With that said, here is some general advice for people thinking about a career in the FBI:

HELPFUL BACKGROUNDS TO HAVE

You can start by looking more in depth at the four entry programs in the FBI: law, accounting, languages, and diversified (which covers everything else). It is no longer true the Bureau is looking primarily for lawyers and accountants. Your strategy ought to focus on what is happening in the country and how the FBI's authority and mission is being reoriented. This is a time of anti-terrorism and global crime. What talents and expertise support this mission? That's right: languages, military experience, the technologies, and the application of both physical and psychological sciences to the courtroom.

Law

All agents need to have a thorough understanding of legal statutes and an ability to read and comprehend legal documents. Obviously, a law degree demonstrates that ability. This specialized entry program is more general than those of accounting or languages, mainly because the Bureau takes pains to thoroughly school all agents in this area. It is, however, an established program for entry into the FBI.

Accounting

Again, the requirements for entering under this specialized program are pretty stringent. You need to have either passed the CPA exam, or have taken enough classes to qualify for it Employment as an accountant and experience on audit engagements is always attractive. This expertise is quite translatable to many FBI investigative functions.

233

Languages

There is always a need for Spanish speakers in the FBI. But the Bureau needs people with proficiency in other languages, as well. Look at immigration and global crime figures right now. Law enforcement agencies will need people who can communicate in Chinese, Bengali, Hindu, and other languages common in those regions. Look at the places around the globe where the United States has political or economic interests. The Mideast is always a hot spot, and the Balkans and other emerging states are quickly becoming allies. Of course, knowing any languages of countries with whom we are allies or at odds regarding terrorist activities is key.

Keep in mind that the FBI test for entering under the language program is extremely rigorous; you really need to be thoroughly fluent in that second language to qualify. But even if you can't make it in under the language program, some foreign-language proficiency can only help you.

Computers

Along with a gun, each new Special Agent is issued his or her own laptop computer. Of course, this is a big change from when I was a new agent. Back then, personal computers didn't exist. I realize that for some of you, that's like saying I rode to work in a horse-and-buggy, but it's true—that's how fast technology is changing. In the late '90s, the FBI engaged an ex-IBM wunderkind to evaluate the FBI's computer technology. Suffice it to say, he wondered how the FBI carried out any of its mission, given the outdated software and hardware.

The computer science needs of the Bureau are three-fold. One, the FBI requires effective professionals to set up and run its internal technology—several Professional Support positions are directed to this need. Second, FBI cases often involve literal computer intrusion matters relating to industrial espionage and national security matters, not to mention financial transactions. Third, the computer is utilized as a means for predators and pedophiles to seduce young victims. As well, criminal targets use it to record financial and operational records and engage in paperless correspondence.

In recent years, the FBI has established advanced technology to handle the above equirements, utilizing the expertise of both Professional Support and Agent personnel. The Bureau has also created investigative and forensic computer squads.

INCREASING YOUR DESIRABLITY

Okay, so you are proficient in one or more of the knowledge sets the FBI is looking for. What can you do with this knowledge to impress upon the Bureau that you are a strong candidate?

Make the Most of Work Experience

The FBI expects applicants to have at least three years of work experience—but of course not all work experience is the same. If you've spent three years folding T-shirts at the Gap, that's not going to be much to draw on. Whatever you do, make a real effort to excel. Volunteer for extra projects; take on more than you are asked to do. Be proactive—create your own opportunities. Naturally, all this is going to be easier if you're doing something you enjoy—another reason to focus on your own talents and abilities.

Hone Your Skills

Think about the basic skills the FBI needs—the ability to communicate in person and on paper, the ability to analyze and organize information, and a certain basic level of physical fitness. How do you measure up in each of these areas? If you're not in great shape, start a fitness program. If you are weak in writing skills, sign up for a class at your local university or community college; if your schedule makes that impractical, colleges all over the country now offer classes via the Internet. You'll probably also find classes that can help build your analytical skills, or you can try any one of dozens of test-prep books designed to help you study for the GRE or the LSAT.

People sometimes ask me about the benefit of other skills—things like self-defense, or CPR, or piloting—that might be related to law enforcement. Are they worth pursuing? Well, if it's something you're interested in, by all means pursue it. But the bottom line is—you're not going to get into the FBI unless your professional skills and experience meet the Bureau's needs. Something like a CPR certification can't hurt, but it's not a make-or-break attribute. It may bump you up a level, but you have to be competitive all around.

Special Agent Owen Smith says, "Say we're hiring pilots—that may be something they immediately see on the application. They focus right in on it, but then they look at the application as a whole. 'Is everything else in place? Does it meet our requirements in other areas?' Just being a pilot may not get you in, but if you were an officer in the military, if you were a plant manager at Nabisco for the last two years—those are pretty attractive things. That makes you competitive with the current pool. And then we see you're a certified pilot, too. So we'll pull you right out of the group to get an interview."

Become Active in Community Service

Now, this isn't the kind of thing that's going to automatically open doors for you. But for someone who is just starting out in their career, community service organizations can offer an opportunity for leadership that might be hard to get at work. And I can guarantee you that the immediate benefits will be tremendous. When I was in the Air Force, finishing up my undergraduate degree, I worked with mentally handicapped kids. It was one of the most rewarding experiences of my life. The FBI looks for maturity, the ability to make good judgements, and the insight to consider "team" first. Whatever you choose, make sure it's something you really support, something you won't resent spending your time doing.

Keep It Clean

The FBI maintains high personal standards for all employees. There's a strict antidrug policy as well as one concerning personal behavior. Maturity is evidenced through good credit ratings, absolutely no criminal record, and other lifestyle choices involving friends, activities, and personal habits. You will undergo a thorough background check. *Thorough* is the operative word. Imagine how those interviewed will describe you, and how these portrayals will look to an employer.

WHAT TO DO IF YOU ARE IN HIGH SCHOOL

Plan to Go to College Right Away

This won't come as a surprise for most of you. With nothing more than a high school diploma, you are probably not going to be able to get the kind of job that will give you meaningful work experience, and you will need a college degree anyway, so why wait? Remember, as I've said several times before, the average applicant age is 31, the median educational level is graduate school, and many individuals have more than the three years of work experience required to submit an application. Those are just the minimum standards —the applicant pool has set the bar a lot higher.

Choose Your Major Carefully

This is most important issue you are facing right now. I'll say it again: Focus on what you want to do. Sure, the FBI is always looking for accounting majors, but if you hate accounting, don't torture yourself for the next seven years—four years of college, plus three years of job experience—on the chance that you'll get into the Bureau in the accounting program.

One important note—If you've told your high school guidance counselor that you are interested in the FBI, he or she might have advised you to major in criminal justice. Well, if you're interested in criminal justice, fine. But don't think this degree leads straight to the Bureau. Owen Smith says, "A criminal justice degree is viewed about the same as a history degree. It's a four-year degree—that's all. It does not get our immediate attention. It's amazing how many candidates tell me that they majored in criminal justice because this is what they were told to do. Unfortunately, a lot of these people are telling me this in their fourth year of college."

A criminal justice degree really prepares you for local law enforcement—working in a police or sheriff's department. Obviously, this will give you experience that can be valuable to the FBI. But if you're really not interested in the front-line aspects of law enforcement, you're much better off choosing another area of study.

Focus on the more stringent disciplines—physics, mathematics, accounting, even a liberal arts degree in philosophy or English will serve you better than a degree in marketing or general studies. Don't opt for an "easy" degree, betting that good grades will help you out. Grades do matter, but not as much as the applicability of your discipline.

Attend the Best School You Can in Your Area of Study

Once you've decided on your major, do some research on the top-ranked schools in that area and apply to those. It can only benefit you. Remember that "name brand" Ivy League schools are not the only options. Just about every school emphasizes a particular area, and you can save tens of thousands of dollars by doing a little research.

But what if the top school in your discipline is Stanford, and you don't get in?

Or you do get in and you can't afford go? Well, don't assume this means you'll never get into the FBI. As far as the Bureau is concerned, your accomplishments mean more than the name of the school on your diploma. The Bureau looks at the total applicant, and what he or she brings to the mission.

Consider an ROTC Program

This isn't an option for everyone, but it can offer several benefits. First, you'll get help paying for college. Second, service as a military officer demonstrates the kind of leadership ability the FBI looks for. Third, the military offers specialized training that is difficult to get in the private sector. So if you have the slightest inclination in this area, give it some serious thought.

WHAT TO DO IF YOU ARE IN COLLEGE

Get the Best Grades You Can

Yes, the FBI focuses on things other than grades. But that doesn't mean grades are meaningless. They are a pretty good measure of your ability to organize your time, analyze information, and complete tasks—all qualities the FBI looks for

Use Your Summers Wisely

I'm not the best poster boy for this; those three high school summers I spent shoveling cow manure didn't do much to prepare me for my later career. However, it was hard work and I made money I used towards school. I always had a plan. Physical labor often brings out the best in a developing adult.

Having said that, many people go out and get a summer internship at an office like the U.S. Customs Service. Treat this like a real job, not just a place to spend time before happy hour. Work hard, put in long hours, and show initiative in taking on projects. You might find out that you really have an aptitude for federal law enforcement; you might take connections with people directly involved in the area you are interested in.

If you can't line up a formal internship for the summer, create one. Think about how you could expand your experience, and offer yourself to a relevant business or organization. Even if you can't afford to take an unpaid internship, carve out some room in your schedule for a part-time volunteer stint. The experience and exposure that you'll get will definitely pay off.

Apply for All the Relevant Internships You Can

Most colleges and universities allow students in most disciplines to earn credit for internships. Check out the policy at your particular school, and research the possibilities. The career counseling center at your school will have a list of local opportunities, and the Internet offers a huge number of resources in this area.

If you qualify, you should definitely apply for the FBI Honors Internship Program. Here are the specifics: At the time of application, you must be an undergraduate in your junior year, or a full-time graduate student. You must plan to return to school after the internship. You also must have a cumulative GPA of 3.0 or above, and be a U.S. citizen. The Bureau is looking for individuals who have demonstrated academic achievement and an interest in law enforcement. The preferred areas of study are engineering, computer science, foreign languages, political science, law, accounting, and the physical sciences.

If you meet the requirements, call the local FBI Field Office and ask for Application Form FD646a. You will also need a current academic transcript, a personal résumé, a recent photograph, a written recommendation from your dean or department head, and a 500-word essay describing your interest in the program. Applications are due on November 1; internships are announced the following spring.

Other FBI Internships

- Special Agent Applicant Processing Unit Non-Paid Internship Program
- FBI Headquarters Personnel Resources Unit Non-Paid Internship Program
- FBI Headquarters Performance Recognition and Awards Unit Non-Paid Internship Program
- National Center for the Anaylsis of Violent Crimes (NCAVC) Non-Paid Internship
- FBI Academy Non-Paid Internship
- Presidential Management Fellows Program (PMFP)

Details regarding these internships can be found on the FBI's offical website at www.fbijobs.gov/intern.asp.

Attend FBI Recruiting Events

Check out the career placement center at your school. Call the nearest FBI Field Office; ask for the Applicant Coordinator and find out when he or she will be at local career days or other events. Realize that as a college student or soon-to-be graduate, you're not ready to apply to the Bureau. But personal contact with an on-board agent will provide you with the most up-to-date information. And if you are as good a candidate as you think you are, the Applicant Coordinator will take note of you

WHAT TO DO IF YOU ARE READY FOR A CAREER CHANGE

Take a Good Look At Your Qualifications

Your big advantage over people who are still in school is that you now have work experience and a list of career accomplishments. Before you submit an application, look at your qualifications. Be ruthlessly honest. Does your work experience dovetail with the investigative needs of the Bureau? Can you point to projects you have headed up and to specific results you have attained? What would your boss say about you if he or she knew you

241

wouldn't find out? Be honest. We all like to think well of ourselves, but there's a difference between self-confidence and self-delusion. The application process is competitive, as I have mentioned several times throughout this text, so begin the process with eyes wide open and make sure you are able to present yourself as a confident and worthy applicant.

Seek Out the Local Applicant Coordinator

Call the local Field Office and find out where the Applicant Coordinator is going to be speaking, what career days he or she is going to be attending. Take that opportunity to present yourself and your qualifications—in an abbreviated form. And listen to what he or she says. If you don't get much encouragement, think hard about whether you want to pursue this. The Applicant Coordinator has no stake in your potential career, one way or another; he or she is trained to be objective. You will get an honest evaluation of your chance from the Bureau's point of view. It's worth paying attention to.

Your recruitment experience will be dictated by your professional demeanor, dress, and attention to detail. Don't go into these offices dressed in shorts and a tube top or t-shirt. Every moment you spend with FBI personnel makes an impression. Every time you speak or write, you are presenting who you are to this organization. Make sure it is the impression you wish to leave with the FBI.

AN INSIDER ACCOUNT

Finally, read what one Applicant Coordinator has to say about the reality of the process.

Owen Smith is the Applicant Coordinator at the Philadelphia Field Office. Here is what he had to say about how applicants first come to the attention of the Bureau.

"There are a lot of people who've always wanted to be an FBI agent, and they either take the initiative and call us, or when we're at a recruiting function—career fairs, what have you—when they're presented with the opportunity to approach us, they seize upon it. We also have individuals, such as Josh, whom I hear about through people I work with, people I know professionally. Personally, I like it when people I know, people I respect in the office here guide me to someone, because I feel those people know what the job entails, and what it takes to succeed in this job. When they tell me here's a good candidate, that gives me some encouragement that there is something here. It's an informed judgment, versus someone calling you on the phone, saying, 'I want to be an FBI agent.'

"Of course, I try to look at everybody the same, but it's a little more encouraging when someone I respect has already had dealings with the person. But the process is completely open. Every person who calls in and says I want to do it is given the same exposure as someone who's personally recommended."

CHAPTER

The Application Process

The FBI is currently in a hiring mode. The FBI has a need for both Special Agents and Professional Support positions. Applying for a job with the FBI isn't like applying for a job at a corporation. For one thing, it takes a whole lot longer. The time it takes will vary from Field Office to Field Office, depending on the pool of applicants at any particular time. But, in general, it will take at least a year from start to finish. Here's the breakdown:

Once you submit your initial application it will take two to three weeks for the Bureau to notify you whether you have been selected for the next phase. If you have been, your letter will give you the date of your initial round of tests—usually six to eight weeks later. After you have taken the written test, you'll again be notified of the results within two to three weeks. If you're approved for a panel interview, that will be scheduled for a date four to six months ahead—if you're a very competitive candidate who is selected from the applicant pool right away. You also might remain in the applicant pool for as long as a year, depending on who else is in that pool. If you pass the panel interview and the written test administered that day, and survive the background check, polygraph, and drug test, you'll be assigned to a new agents' class beginning in about six months.

Once you get into the process, you will have contact with the applicant coordinator at your Field Office who can answer any questions you will have. Most of the following information will apply to the earlier stages of the process.

INITIAL APPLICATION STRATEGY

Identify the Requirements for the Job You Want

Special Agent: The minimum requirements are listed in chapter 7.

Professional Support Personnel: Requirements vary tremendously, depending on the job. Call the FBI Field Office nearest you (refer to page xxx for a list of all 56 Field Offices and their contact informaion) and ask for the requirements brochure for the specific job you are interested in. If you're not sure of a specific job title, ask for a general category—Forensic Support Personnel, for example.

Obtain the Forms You Will Need

Special Agent: Call the Field Office nearest you to get an application, or download the application from the FBI's web site at www.fbi.gov.

Professional Support Personnel: Again, because there are so many different jobs, you'll need to get the right application for the job you want. Call the Field Office nearest you.

Whether you're applying for a job as a Special Agent or in the support area, don't try to hide anything on your application. Tell the truth. This is how Doug Rhoads puts it: "Candor is always much more productive than evasion. Say you've got a gap on your résumé. You spent six months on the beach at Pensacola, just taking a break. Well, so what? As long as everything else checks out, who cares? But an applicant cannot survive a lack-of-candor issue."

Top-notch skills which match what the Bureau needs might outweigh what seems to be a blemish in your record. On the other hand, if the blemish is significant—"I have a six-month gap in my résumé because I was in jail on a DWI"—the FBI isn't the place for you, no matter what your skills are.

Submit Your Application—and Wait

You don't get points for following up your application with a phone call; in fact, calling the Field Office to ask about the status of your application could send the wrong signal. Within three weeks of submitting your initial application, you will receive a response from the FBI. You will be told one of two things: You've been scheduled for the next stage of the application process, the written test, or you're considered "not competitive" with other current applicants. If you submit an application and don't hear back within three weeks, then go ahead and call, just to confirm that your application was received. Otherwise, just sit tight.

FREQUENTLY ASKED QUESTIONS

If I'm rejected at this stage of the process, will I find out why?

The standard notification simply states that you've been found "not competitive" with the other candidates applying at the same time. If you have some personal connection with an on-board agent, talk to her about what might have happened. You can also ask to speak to the applicant coordinator at the local Field Office, but remember that it is strictly up to him or her to decide whether to discuss your application with you. Remember, Applicant Coordinators and their personalities will vary. Try to assess what the expectations are from this person. Some say telephone calls are okay, and some discourage them.And there may not be much information the applicant coordinator can give you. Owen Smith says, "Sometimes it's something the applicant coordinator can articulate because it's a very basic issue. A person who just got out of college, or a college grad who's been working for three years, but he's been working all that time as a clerk in a convenience store—it's very easy to say to him, 'Your experience is not conducive to the current needs of the Bureau.' That's a very clear-cut thing. But if someone has three, four, five years of managerial experience, but he or she's just not competitive with everyone else in the pool—according to policy, the applicant coordinator does not comment on specific FBI HQ decisions."

And also keep in mind that even if the Applicant Coordinator or your contact in the Bureau gives you feedback about a specific problem with your application, correcting that problem is no guarantee that you'll get in the next time you apply. Smith says, "By the time you go out and do what you needed to do to make yourself more competitive with the original pool of applicants, you are competing against a whole new pool of people."

Is there a limit to the number of times I can apply?

At this stage, no. But if you apply several times, after making a real effort to correct any deficiencies you've been able to identify, and you still don't succeed, then you should refocus your efforts.

Once you advance to the next stage, limits do go into effect. You're allowed to take the three-part written test twice and you're allowed to sit for the panel interview twice. But if you can't make it through the process by then, you're out.

Will my application be held on file?

Again, at this stage, no. If you make it through the written test, your application may be held for as long as a year before you're called up for a panel interview. It depends on how competitive you are with the other applicants. The Applicant Coordinator at the Field Office through which you apply will keep you informed.

248

THE STANDARDIZED TEST

Once you've made it through the initial cut, you'll be scheduled for a three-part standardized test. When you are notified of the date of your test, you'll also be given a study guide. I strongly recommend that you go beyond this study guide when you're preparing for the test. You will need to demonstrate mathematical ability, so brush up on your algebra. If it's been a while since you've taken a standardized test, refresh yourself on basic test-taking strategy—how to organize your time, what to do if you get stuck.

This test is divided into three sections:

The Biodata Inventory

You're given 45 minutes to answer 47 questions. The test is intended to measure the following: your ability to organize, plan, and prioritize; your ability to maintain a positive image; your ability to evaluate information and make judgments; your initiative and motivation; your ability to adapt to changing situations; and your ability to meet the physical requirements.

This is a fairly standard personal-assessment test. You're expected to answer questions as they apply to you. Special Agent Owen Smith provided the following example:

> In connection with your work, in which of the following have you taken the most pride?
>
> A. Having been able to avoid any major controversies
> B. Having gotten where you are on your own
> C. Having been able to work smoothly with people
> D. Having provided a lot of new ideas, good or bad
> E. Having been able to do well, no matter what management requested"

The Cognitive Ability Test

This is where you will need your algebra. This section of the test, measuring your mathematical ability, is divided into three parts:

- Mathematical reasoning—29 minutes to answer 25 questions
- Ability to interpret data in tables and graphs—24 minutes to answer 25 questions
- Ability to learn mathematical relationships—22 minutes to answer 25 questions

Taken together, the three test areas are designed to measure mathematical reasoning, data and analytical interpretation skills, mathematical knowledge, ability to attend to detail, and ability to evaluate information and make decisions.

The Situational Judgment Test

You're given 33 problem situations and 90 minutes to answer questions about how you'd handle the situations. This section is designed to measure: your ability to organize, plan, and prioritize; your ability to relate to others effectively; your ability to maintain a positive image; your ability to evaluate information and use your judgment to make decisions; your ability to adapt to changing situations, and your integrity.

Here's an example of this type of question that Owen Smith provided:

> You are shopping when you notice a man robbing the store. What would you do?
>
> A. Leave the store as quickly as possible and call the police
> B. Try to apprehend the robber yourself
> C. Follow the man and call the police as soon as he seems settled somewhere
> D. Nothing, as you do not wish to get involved in the situation

With the situational judgment and biodata inventory sections, you may be tempted to fudge your answers—marking the responses you think the FBI is looking for, rather than the ones that really apply to you. Not a good idea. There's no way to do that kind of second-guessing consistently, and you'll end up with answers that are all over the map. The test won't reflect who you are, and what it seems to show probably won't be all that attractive. Smith says, "You're better off taking your chances with your honest answers than you are trying to out-think the test. You probably have more of a chance of giving yourself a shot at it that way."

THE PANEL INTERVIEW

Once you take the standardized test, the results are analyzed and you're notified whether or not you can proceed to the next phase of the application process. This is where the real pressure kicks in. Owen Smith says, "The three-part test is just a key to open the door; once that door is open, the written test has no bearing on anything. You are then strictly on your own. It's up to your ability to compete with others on the interview."

Your panel interview could be scheduled as soon as four months after your standardized test, or it could take up to a year. You and several other applicants from the same region will be scheduled for your interviews on the same day.

Each applicant will also take a written exam. Some applicants will be scheduled for the interview first; others will take the exam first. This exam consists of a single problem—a scenario you're expected to analyze and respond to. Unlike the standardized test, this is an open-ended exam. You're expected to read and evaluate the scenario, formulate a response, and write out your answer. You're given a specific length of time in which to respond; that time period may change from test to test. One recent applicant offered this example: "It was something like this: You're a journalist researching a story. While you're doing your research, you find out all this information about another situation. You have to write a memo to your editor, convincing him that there's a story in this new situation and you need to be able to pursue it."

The panel interview is administered by three assessors, Special Agents who primarily work in the field. The assessors receive training in conducting the interviews and evaluating applicants' answers. They're given 15 questions to ask each applicant; the wording and order of the questions remain the same for each applicant. Those questions are formulated by the recruiting office at FBI Headquarters, and revised about once a year. Each time the questions are revised, the assessors throughout the country go through another training session.

When you walk into the interview room, the assessors know two things about you: your name and your Social Security number. They don't know how you did on the earlier tests, what you do for a living, or who you listed as references. Your performance in that room, on that day, is all the assessors care about. Owen Smith says, "You're always going to have some element of subjectivity, but whole process is designed to be as objective as possible. That's why the assessors receive that training; that's why they're given certain keys to evaluate answers. We really try to take out as much of the subjectivity as possible, realizing there's always the human element. But that's why the applicant has a blank slate when they walk in."

During the interview as a whole, you're going to be evaluated on your ability to communicate orally. Specific questions are designed to test your ability to organize, plan, and prioritize; your ability to relate effectively with others; your ability to maintain a positive image; your ability to evaluate information and make judgment decisions; your initiative and motivation; your ability to adapt to changing situations; your integrity; and your ability to meet physical requirements. Throughout the interview, the assessors take detailed notes; the entire interview is also tape recorded.

After the interview is concluded, the assessors come up with individual ratings for the applicant, then discuss their responses to come up with a consensus rating. Everything from the interview—the assessors' notes, the tape, the rating forms—is sent to FBI Headquarters to become part of the applicant's file.

THE BACKGROUND CHECK

The first step in the FBI's background check involves following up your paper trail. This happens fairly early in the process, just to weed out the obviously unsuitable people. They'll look up your school transcripts, your credit report, your medical history, and any military or arrest record.

The more intensive background check occurs later in the process, after you've already cleared several hurdles. Sending retired Agents like me out on these investigations gets expensive, and the Bureau doesn't want to waste money checking up on people that are just going to wash out on some other point.

The face-to-face interviews begin with the references and employers you've listed. The investigators ask the kinds of questions any employer would ask—how your work performance was, what kind of student you were, that sort of thing. There's nothing especially tricky about the questions. Go ahead and tell your references that you're applying for a job with the FBI, you've listed them as references, and they might be getting a visit from some people with badges.

Doug Rhoads has conducted a few of these background investigations, and he recommends that you notify your references. "Tell people they're likely to get a visit. It'll make things easier, and it's not like there's anything undercover about the investigation, anyway. When I go see people, I show them my I.D. and my credentials. I say right up front, 'My name's Doug Rhoads, I'm an FBI Special Investigator, and I'm here to conduct a background investigation on so-and-so for employment with the FBI.' Then there's two statements I make very clearly up front. I let them know, 'This is not a criminal matter. So-and-so is being considered for employment as a Special Agent,' or whatever the position is. Then I tell them, 'Under the Freedom of Information Act, if there's anything you say to me that you wish to be treated as confidential, all you have to do is express that wish to me.' That's to elicit candor. The applicant can have access to whatever's in the file, unless the interviewees specifically request confidentiality. And we want the interviewees to feel like they can be honest without having it come back to them."

Of course, the investigators will gather other sources, too. There's no way you can alert every single person the FBI will speak to—which is really the point of a background check. But unless you had significant trouble with former neighbors, employers, or close relations, you shouldn't have anything to worry about.

This is how Doug describes it: "Painting a complete picture—that's what the background is for. The truth of it is, the biggest reason people are knocked out during the background check isn't because we find out they've been selling drugs or anything like that. It's poor work performance. The former boss says, 'No, this person really wasn't the best employee. There were these incidents where he didn't deliver.' The applicant just wasn't as good as he thought he was.

"It's not the little old lady next door saying, 'Oh, there were all kinds of wild parties over there. They were such heavy drinkers, they'd drink a whole six-pack a week over there.' And you're thinking, 'Oh my God, four people going through a six-pack.' You've got to put it into perspective. 'They were loud twice a month'—that's not going to keep you from getting hired."

Believe it or not, FBI agents were young once, too.

POLYGRAPH FAQS

If you've never had a polygraph, the idea of taking one can be intimidating. How does it work? What are they going to ask about? What if I'm nervous during the test? Can I beat the polygraph?

254

Well, here are the answers:

How does it work?

The polygraph measures several involuntary physiological responses to stress—specifically, the stress involved in lying. When you're actually "hooked up," you'll be seated in a chair near the polygraph. Three sensors will be attached:

- A blood pressure cuff, to measure heart rate
- Convoluted rubber tubes, around the abdomen and chest, to measure respiratory activity
- Two small metal plates, attached to the fingers, to measure sweat gland activity.

The questioning phase also has three parts:

Pretest. Before you're hooked up to the polygraph, the examiner asks you several questions. There are the baseline questions—"Is your name Jane Doe? Were you born in Peoria, Illinois?" Then there are the real questions— questions such as "Have you ever manufactured, transported, or sold illegal drugs?" You're not going to lie about your name or where you were born; even if your heart is beating faster than it normally would because you're nervous, that elevated heart rate is going to register as the baseline for the test.

Chart Collection Phase. You're then hooked up to the polygraph, and the examiner goes through the questions again. Then, there's the follow-up— "Did you lie when you told me you haven't manufactured, transported or sold illegal drugs?" This is the key to the use of the polygraph—the specific questioning and the immediate response.

Test Data Analysis Phase. The examiner reviews the charts and notes areas where deception is indicated. When appropriate, the examiner will ask the subject to explain or clarify unusual physiological responses—something along the lines of, "You seemed to react strongly to the questions about theft. Is there a specific reason for that?"

What are they going to ask about?

The FBI maintains very high ethical standards among its employees. Even so, they're not looking for saints, or robots. Drug use isn't defined as being in the same room as a marijuana cigarette; theft isn't defined as making a few personal phone calls on company time.

The questions on a polygraph are very carefully designed to be limited and specific, and thus useful. Doug Rhoads says, "You're not asked things like, 'Have you ever stolen a pen from work?' Give me a break. The questions also can't be as broad as 'Have you ever … ?' That's why the pretest is so important. You'll be asked, 'Did you lie to the examiner when you said you've never significantly defrauded your employer?' It must be specific. The broad, 'have you ever' questions will always show deception because the subject doesn't know exactly what you mean. 'Well, maybe that box of pens counts as significant fraud.' You've got to narrow it down to get the meaningful deceptions." Many questions often have to do with truthfulness on your application to the FBI including the drug use self-report. Remember, candor is everything.

What if the polygraph shows I'm lying when I'm not?

During the pretest, the examiner will assess the subject's emotional state and physical condition and allow for any effect these might have. The control questions help identify subjects who are extremely responsive or extremely nervous; there are specialized tests for use in these circumstances. The examiners make every effort to get an accurate reading from the polygraph.

If you know a deceptive response on your polygraph is inaccurate, you can request a second polygraph with a second examiner, or you can ask to have the first polygraph reviewed by another examiner.

As far as trying to beat the polygraph, forget it. It's not the machine you're trying to fool, it's the examiner—and a skilled, experienced polygraph examiner is almost impossible to fool. Doug Rhoads says, "We've got examiners here in Charlottesville who are so good—say I've got you on the machine, and you lay out six cards in front of you. You pick up one card. It's the six of hearts. Then you rearrange the cards, keeping your eye on the six of hearts. Then I'll rearrange them. Slowly; this is not a trick. You know exactly where the six of hearts is. I'll have you put your hand on each card and the examiner asks you, 'Is that the six of hearts? Is that the six of hearts?' You say no to all of them. And he can tell you from the machine which one you lied on. You just can't control your body. You know that's the six of hearts and you're saying no. And that's not even a lie that you care anything about. Your responses are going to be even more obvious on a big lie."

No offense to Doug's examiners down in Charlottesville, but I'm sure the people at the FBI are at least as good.

DRUG TEST

This is a standard urine test that screens for opiates and THC, or marijuana by-products. Along with the polygraph, this test is designed to ensure that applicants adhere to the strict no-drugs policy. Nothing to worry about if you don't indulge.

* * * * * *

FINAL ADVICE

Your first step is to evaluate your current background and those qualities consistent with an FBI career. Call your nearest FBI Division and speak directly with the Applicant Coordinator.

The completion of the application is the next step. The application should be typed. Leave no information unaddressed—the information requested is absolutely necessary to consider you an FBI employee. Select your references carefully; know what they will say about you prior to listing them. Detail your employment and schooling carefully. The manner in which you fill out this application is the FBI's first look at how you present yourself. This isn't an application for a summer job—many applicants have cross-outs, misspellings, and other problems on their applications. This is not a good image to communicate at the outset.

The way you speak and the way you write are vital to the professional image you project. If your handwriting is awful, type it. If you can't spell, proofread. And it goes without saying your information should be absolutely accurate. Don't guess; that only communicates laziness.

Be current-event saavy. Be able to converse intelligently about world affairs. You are not expected to be a sycophant and say what you think the FBI wants to hear. Communicate well-informed opinions with depth and confidence.

Lastly, humility is a wonderful quality. This does not mean you should not sell yourself and put your best foot forward. It does mean the world does not revolve around you and, more importantly, that you are looking to contribute to a large and important effort.

So now you know more about what it takes to become an FBI agent, and what kind of career you could expect to have. If you decide to go for it, I wish you the best of luck. I believe it is an incredible honor and privilege to be a member of the finest law enforcement agency in the world.

PART FIVE

Appendixes

Sample Salary Charts

Most FBI white-collar employees are paid according to the General Schedule contained in Title 5, U.S. Code, Section 53332(A). Some General Schedule personnel in specialized or competitive job categories are paid at a higher level under a Special Pay Rate System. In addition, special geographic locality rates may apply; therefore, the pay scales used in different parts of the country vary. The highest-ranking FBI personnel are paid under the SES Schedule or the Executive Schedule.

On the following page is a 2005 schedule for entry positions (while assigned to Quantico for example). The table following is a pay schedule for the Atlanta metropolitan area. Finally, the table following is a pay schedule for the New York metropolitan area.

SALARY TABLE NO. 491

LAW ENFORCEMENT OFFICERS

EFFECTIVE JANUARY 2005

Grade	Step 1	Step 2	Step 3	Step 4	Step 5	Step 6	Step 7	Step 8	Step 9	Step 10	WGI
3	23577	24232	24887	25542	26197	26852	27507	28162	28817	29472	655
4	26466	27201	27936	28671	29406	30141	30876	31611	32346	33081	735
5	30438	31261	32084	32907	33730	34553	35376	36199	37022	37845	823
6	32092	33009	33926	34843	35760	36677	37594	38511	39428	40345	917
7	34643	35662	36681	37700	38719	39738	40757	41776	42795	43814	1019
8	36108	37236	38364	39492	40620	41748	42876	44004	45132	46260	1128
9	38636	39882	41128	42374	43620	44866	46112	47358	48604	49850	1246
10	42548	43921	45294	46667	48040	49413	50786	52159	53532	54905	1373

Salary Table 2005-ATL
INCORPORATING THE 2.50% GENERAL SCHEDULE INCREASE AND A LOCALITY PAYMENT OF 13.87%

FOR THE LOCALITY PAY AREA OF ATLANTA-SANDY SPRINGS-GAINESVILLE, GA-AL

EFFECTIVE JANUARY 2005
Annual Rates by Grade and Step

Grade	Step 1	Step 2	Step 3	Step 4	Step 5	Step 6	Step 7	Step 8	Step 9	Step 10
1	18237	18845	19452	20056	20663	21019	21617	22222	22247	22815
2	20505	20992	21671	22247	22495	23157	23818	24480	25141	25803
3	22372	23118	23864	24610	25355	26101	26847	27593	28339	29085
4	25115	25952	26789	27626	28463	29300	30137	30974	31811	32648
5	28100	29037	29974	30911	31848	32785	33723	34660	35597	36534
6	31322	32366	33411	34455	35499	36543	37587	38632	39676	40720
7	34807	35967	37127	38288	39448	40608	41769	42929	44089	45250
8	38547	39832	41116	42401	43685	44970	46254	47538	48823	50107
9	42576	43995	45414	46832	48251	49670	51089	52508	53927	55345
10	46886	48449	50013	51576	53140	54703	56267	57830	59393	60957
11	51514	53231	54948	56665	58382	60099	61817	63534	65251	66968
12	61741	63799	65857	67914	69972	72030	74087	76145	78202	80260
13	73421	75868	78315	80762	83209	85656	88103	90551	92998	95445
14	86761	89653	92546	95438	98330	101222	104115	107007	109899	112792
15	102056	105458	108861	112263	115666	119068	122471	125873	129275	132678

Salary Table 2005-NY
INCORPORATING THE 2.50% GENERAL SCHEDULE INCREASE AND A LOCALITY PAYMENT OF 20.99%

FOR THE LOCALITY PAY AREA OF NEW YORK-NEWARK-BRIDGEPORT, NY-NJ-CT-PA

EFFECTIVE JANUARY 2005
Annual Rates by Grade and Step

Grade	Step 1	Step 2	Step 3	Step 4	Step 5	Step 6	Step 7	Step 8	Step 9	Step 10
1	19378	20024	20669	21310	21955	22334	22969	23611	23638	24242
2	21787	22305	23026	23638	23902	24605	25307	26010	26713	27416
3	23771	24563	25356	26148	26941	27733	28526	29318	30111	30903
4	26686	27575	28464	29353	30243	31132	32021	32910	33800	34689
5	29857	30852	31848	32844	33840	34835	35831	36827	37823	38818
6	33281	34390	35500	36609	37719	38828	39938	41047	42157	43266
7	36983	38216	39449	40682	41915	43147	44380	45613	46846	48079
8	40958	42322	43687	45052	46417	47781	49146	50511	51876	53240
9	45238	46746	48253	49761	51268	52776	54283	55791	57298	58806
10	49818	51479	53140	54801	56462	58124	59785	61446	63107	64768
11	54735	56559	58384	60208	62033	63857	65682	67506	69331	71155
12	65602	67788	69975	72161	74347	76533	78720	80906	83092	85279
13	78012	80612	83212	85812	88412	91012	93612	96212	98813	101413
14	92186	95259	98332	101405	104478	107552	110625	113698	116771	119844
15	108437	112052	115668	119283	122898	126513	130128	133744	137359	140300

APPENDIX

FBI Field Offices

Albany Field Office
Federal Bureau of Investigation
200 McCarty Avenue
Albany, New York 12209
(518) 465-7551
http://albany.fbi.gov

Albuquerque Field Office
Federal Bureau of Investigation
4200 Luecking Park Ave. NE
Albuquerque, New Mexico 87107
(505) 889-1300
http://albuquerque.fbi.gov

Anchorage Field Office
Federal Bureau of Investigation
101 East Sixth Avenue
Anchorage, Alaska 99501
(907) 258-5322
http://anchorage.fbi.gov

Atlanta Field Office
Federal Bureau of Investigation, Suite 400
2635 Century Parkway, N.E.
Atlanta, Georgia 30345
(404) 679-9000
http://atlanta.fbi.gov

Baltimore Field Office
Federal Bureau of Investigation
2600 Lord Baltimore
Baltimore, Maryland 21244
(410) 265-8080
http://baltimore.fbi.gov

Birmingham Field Office
Federal Bureau of Investigation, Room 1400
2121 8th Avenue N.
Birmingham, Alabama 35203
(205) 326-6166
http://birmingham.fbi.gov

Appendixes

Boston Field Office
Federal Bureau of Investigation
Suite 600
One Center Plaza
Boston, Massachusetts 02108
(617) 742-5533
http://boston.fbi.gov

Buffalo Field Office
Federal Bureau of Investigation
One FBI Plaza
Buffalo, New York 14202
(716) 856-7800
http://buffalo.fbi.gov

Charlotte Field Office
Federal Bureau of Investigation
Suite 900
400 South Tryon Street
Charlotte, North Carolina 28285
(704) 377-9200
http://charlotte.fbi.gov

Chicago Field Office
Federal Bureau of Investigation
Room 905
E. M. Dirksen Federal Office Building
219 South Dearborn Street
Chicago, Illinois 60604
(312) 431-1333
http://chicago.fbi.gov

Cincinnati Field Office
Federal Bureau of Investigation
Room 9000
550 Main Street
Cincinnati, Ohio 45202
(513) 421-4310
http://cincinnati.fbi.gov

Cleveland Field Office
Federal Bureau of Investigation
Federal Office Building
1501 Lakeside Avenue
Cleveland, Ohio 44114
(216) 522-1400
http://cleveland.fbi.gov

Columbia Field Office
Federal Bureau of Investigation
151 Westpark Blvd.
Columbia, South Carolina 29210
(803) 551-4200
http://columbia.fbi.gov

Dallas Field Office
Federal Bureau of Investigation
One Justice Way
Dallas, Texas 75220
(972) 559-5000
http://dallas.fbi.gov

Denver Field Office
Federal Bureau of Investigation
Federal Office Building, Suite 1823
1961 Stout Street, 18th Floor
Denver, Colorado 80294
(303) 629-7171
http://denver.fbi.gov

Detroit Field Office
Federal Bureau of Investigation
26th Floor, P. V. McNamara FOB
477 Michigan Avenue
Detroit, Michigan 48226
(313) 965-2323
http://detroit.fbi.gov

El Paso Field Office
Federal Bureau of Investigation
660 South Mesa Hills
Suite 3000
El Paso, Texas 79912
(915) 832-5000
http://elpaso.fbi.gov

Honolulu Field Office
Federal Bureau of Investigation
Room 4-230, Kalanianaole EOB
300 Ala Moana Boulevard
Honolulu, Hawaii 96850
(808) 566-4300
http://honolulu.fbi.gov

Houston Field Office
Federal Bureau of Investigation
Suite 200
2500 East TC Jester
Houston, Texas 77008
(713) 693-5000
http://houston.fbi.gov

Indianapolis Field Office
Federal Bureau of Investigation
Room 679, FOB
575 North Pennsylvania Street
Indianapolis, Indiana 46204
(317) 639-3301
http://indianapolis.fbi.gov

Jackson Field Office
Federal Bureau of Investigation
Room 1553, FOB
100 West Capitol Street
Jackson, Mississippi 39269
(601) 948-5000
http://jackson.fbi.gov

Jacksonville Field Office
Federal Bureau of Investigation
Suite 200
7820 Arlington Expressway
Jacksonville, Florida 32211
(904) 721-1211
http://jacksonville.fbi.gov

Kansas City Field Office
Federal Bureau of Investigation
1300 Summit
Kansas City, Missouri 64105-1362
(816) 512-8200
http://kansascity.fbi.gov

Knoxville Field Office
Federal Bureau of Investigation
Suite 600, John J. Duncan FOB
710 Locust Street
Knoxville, Tennessee 37902
(423) 544-0751
http://knoxville.fbi.gov

Las Vegas Field Office
Federal Bureau of Investigation
John Lawrence Bailey Building
700 East Charleston Boulevard
Las Vegas, Nevada 89104
(702) 385-1281
http://lasvegas.fbi.gov

Little Rock Field Office
Federal Bureau of Investigation
Suite 200
Two Financial Centre
10825 Financial Centre Parkway
Little Rock, Arkansas 72211
(501) 221-9100
http://littlerock.fbi.gov

Appendixes

Los Angeles Field Office
Federal Bureau of Investigation
Suite 1700, FOB
11000 Wilshire Boulevard
Los Angeles, California 90024
(310) 477-6565
http://losangeles.fbi.gov

Louisville Field Office
Federal Bureau of Investigation
Room 500
600 Martin Luther King Jr. Place
Louisville, Kentucky 40202
(502) 583-3941
http://louisville.fbi.gov

Memphis Field Office
Federal Bureau of Investigation
Suite 3000, Eagle Crest Building
225 North Humphreys Boulevard
Memphis, Tennessee 38120
(901) 747-4300
http://memphis.fbi.gov

Miami Field Office
Federal Bureau of Investigation
16320 Northwest Second Avenue
North Miami Beach, Florida 33169
(305) 944-9101
http://miami.fbi.gov

Milwaukee Field Office
Federal Bureau of Investigation
Suite 600
330 East Kilbourn Avenue
Milwaukee, Wisconsin 53202-6627
(414) 276-4684
http://milwaukee.fbi.gov

Minneapolis Field Office
Federal Bureau of Investigation
Suite 1100
111 Washington Avenue, South
Minneapolis, Minnesota 55401
(612) 376-3200
http://minneapolis.fbi.gov

Mobile Field Office
Federal Bureau of Investigation
One St. Louis Center
200 N. Royal Street
Mobile, Alabama 36602
(251) 438-3674
http://mobile.fbi.gov

Newark Field Office
Federal Bureau of Investigation
1 Gateway Center
Newark, New Jersey 07102
(973) 792-3000
http://newark.fbi.gov

New Haven Field Office
Federal Bureau of Investigation
600 State Street
New Haven, Connecticut 06511
(203) 777-6311
http://newhaven.fbi.gov

New Orleans Field Office
Federal Bureau of Investigation
2901 Leon C. Simon Drive
New Orleans, Louisiana 70126
(504) 816-3000
http://neworleans.fbi.gov

New York Field Office
Federal Bureau of Investigation
26 Federal Plaza, 23rd Floor
New York, New York 10278
(212) 384-1000
http://newyork.fbi.gov

Norfolk Field Office
Federal Bureau of Investigation
150 Corporate Boulevard
Norfolk, Virginia 23502
(757) 455-0100
http://norfolk.fbi.gov

Oklahoma City Field Office
Federal Bureau of Investigation
3301 West Memorial Drive
Oklahoma City, Oklahoma 73134
(405) 290-7770
http://oklahomacity.fbi.gov

Omaha Field Office
Federal Bureau of Investigation
10755 Burt Street
Omaha, Nebraska 68114
(402) 493-8688
http://omaha.fbi.gov

Philadelphia Field Office
Federal Bureau of Investigation
8th Floor
William J. Green Jr. FOB
600 Arch Street
Philadelphia, Pennsylvania 19106
(215) 418-4000
http://philadelphia.fbi.gov

Phoenix Field Office
Federal Bureau of Investigation
Suite 400
201 East Indianola Avenue
Phoenix, Arizona 85012
(602) 279-5511
http://phoenix.fbi.gov

Pittsburgh Field Office
Federal Bureau of Investigation
3311 East Carlson Street
Pittsburgh, Pennsylvania 15203
(412) 432-4000
http://pittsburgh.fbi.gov

Portland Field Office
Federal Bureau of Investigation
Suite 400, Crown Plaza Building
1500 Southwest 1st Avenue
Portland, Oregon 97201
(503) 224-4181
http://portland.fbi.gov

Richmond Field Office
Federal Bureau of Investigation
1970 East Parham Road
Richmond, Virginia 23228
(804) 261-1044
http://richmond.fbi.gov

Sacramento Field Office
Federal Bureau of Investigation
4500 Orange Grove Avenue
Sacramento, California 95841-4205
(916) 481-9110
http://sacramento.fbi.gov

Appendixes

St. Louis Field Office
Federal Bureau of Investigation
2222 Market Street
St. Louis, Missouri 63103
(314) 231-4324
http://stlouis.fbi.gov

Salt Lake City Field Office
Federal Bureau of Investigation
Suite 1200
257 East, 200 South
Salt Lake City, Utah 84111
(801) 579-1400
http://saltlakecity.fbi.gov

San Antonio Field Office
Federal Bureau of Investigation Suite 200
U.S. Post Office Courthouse Building
615 East Houston Street
San Antonio, Texas 78205
(210) 225-6741
http://sanantonio.fbi.gov

San Diego Field Office
Federal Bureau of Investigation
Federal Office Building
9797 Aero Drive
San Diego, California 92123-1800
(619) 565-1255
http://sandiego.fbi.gov

San Francisco Field Office
Federal Bureau of Investigation
450 Golden Gate Avenue
13th Floor
San Francisco, California 94102
(415) 553-7400
http://sanfrancisco.fbi.gov

San Juan Field Office
Federal Bureau of Investigation
Room 526, U.S. Federal Building
150 Carlos Chardon Avenue
Hato Rey San Juan, Puerto Rico 00918-1716
(787) 754-6000
http://sanjuan.fbi.gov

Seattle Field Office
Federal Bureau of Investigation
1110 Third Avenue
Seattle, Washington 98101
(206) 622-0460
http://seattle.fbi.gov

Springfield Field Office
Federal Bureau of Investigation
Suite 400
400 West Monroe Street
Springfield, Illinois 62704
(217) 522-9675
http://springfield.fbi.gov

Tampa Field Office
Federal Bureau of Investigation
Suite 510, FOB
500 Zack Street
Tampa, Florida 33602
(813) 273-4566
http://tampa.fbi.gov

Washington Metropolitan
Field Office
Federal Bureau of Investigation
601 4th Street NW
Washington, D.C. 20535
(202) 278-2000
http://washingtondc.fbi.gov

Notes

Notes

Notes

Notes

Notes

Notes

Notes

Notes

Introducing a smarter way to learn.

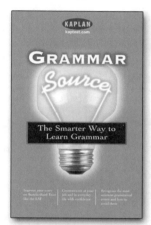

- Focused, practice-based learning
- Concepts for everyday life
- Recognition and recall exercises
- Quizzes throughout